What Orwell Didn't Know

Propaganda and
the New Face
of American Politics

Edited by
ANDRÁS SZÁNTÓ

With an Introduction by
ORVILLE SCHELL

PUBLICAFFAIRS
New York

Library of Congress Cataloging-in-Publication Data
    What Orwell didn't know : propaganda and the new face of American politics / edited
by András Szántó ; with an introduction by Orville Schell. — 1st ed.
    p. cm.
    Includes bibliographical references.
    ISBN–13: 978–1–58648–560–3 (pbk.)
    ISBN–10: 1–58648–560–1 (pbk.)
    1. Propaganda—United States. 2. Mass media and propaganda—United States. 3.
United States—Politics and government. 4. Orwell, George, 1903–1950. Politics and the
English language. I. Szántó, András.
    HM1231.W43 2007
    303.3'750973—dc22

                                                                              2007036728

First Edition

10 9 8 7 6 5 4 3 2 1

What Orwell
Didn't Know

CONTENTS

CONTENTS

Part Two:
Symbols and Battlegrounds

CONTENTS

Part Three:
Media and Message

András Szántó

Every book has a story. The story of this anthology began when the deans of five prominent journalism schools got together to do something about the state of public debate in America. They were worried about what was happening to political language, which seemed to be divorcing itself from reality at an alarming rate. They were especially concerned about the waning power—or inclination—of the press to bring political rhetoric in line with facts. By coincidence, these concerns were being voiced around the sixtieth anniversary of the publication of George Orwell's classic essay, "Politics and the English Language" (1946). Orwell offered a convenient jumping-off point for the conversations that followed, and eventually, for the essays in this book. His jeremiad on the corrosion of language and the corruption of politics—two phenomena that he saw going hand in hand, the one reinforcing the other—echoed with renewed importance in the United States of the early twenty-first century.

Plans were soon underway for a conference at the New York Public Library, timed to overlap with the publication of this book. The premise of this anthology is that there is something categorically different about how messages are framed and re-framed in today's American politics; that while the admonishments in "Politics and the English Language" (see Appendix) still ring true, the terms of debate have also shifted in ways that might have surprised or even baffled Orwell. It goes without saying that politicians have always taken liberties with the truth. Rhetoric and persuasion are inseparable from public life. Skeptics may point out that politics has less to do with honesty than with the deft pursuit of power or compromise. Even so, it's too easy to explain away the yawning gap between rhetoric and reality by simply asserting: It has ever been thus.

Asking "What Orwell Didn't Know" is a timely exercise. The United States is the most powerful democracy in the world; yet its lavishly funded industries of political messaging and image making are unrivaled in their scale and technical wizardry. Americans enjoy open access to an astonishing array of information; yet they are bombarded with so many messages, and diverted by such mesmerizing amusements, that millions tune out from politics altogether. The creative and commercial zeal of the mass media are breathtaking; yet there is widespread concern about the ability of news organizations, in particular, to render an accurate, independent record of what politicians are doing. America's military adventure in Iraq taps into all these worrisome symptoms.

There are many takes on George Orwell between these covers, yet it is important to underscore that this is not a symposium on Orwell, or on his essay on language and politics, or, for that matter, on his apocalyptic novel, *1984*, which persistently rears its head. Rather, our aim was to assemble a group of journalists and experts from various fields to chart the complex topography of propaganda within the new landscape of American politics.

David Rieff and Nicholas Lemann focus on points of convergence and divergence between the political culture of Orwell's day and our own. Francine Prose, Mark Danner, Aryeh Neier, and Patricia Williams delve into contemporary language to discover intentional or merely careless slippages of meaning that obfuscate political perceptions. Several writers take us back to turning points in the annals of propaganda: Orville Schell recounts China's experiments in mind control, Konstanty Gebert reports from post-Communist Poland, and Frances FitzGerald looks back on arguably the most successful endeavor in modern American spin, the selling of Star Wars.

Ideology and science are commingling with public discourse in some ways that Orwell, in 1946, certainly could not have foreseen. Susan Harding outlines the often ingenious methods that the religious right has employed to "revoice" mainstream media practices. Alice O'Connor takes us into the world of politically financed think tanks, which manufacture pseudo-social science that makes it possible for ideology to masquerade as fact. Two experts of language and the mind, George Lakoff and Drew Westen, explain how scientific advances in our knowledge of the brain, and specifically, the cognitive and emotional processes underlying voter behavior, are reshaping campaign messages and strategies.

The latter part of the book concerns itself chiefly with journalism. Geoffrey Cowan, Victor Navasky, and Martin Kaplan offer close-up views of the news media's challenges: from agonized decisionmaking in newsrooms about how to respond to spin, to the consequences of recent media legislation, to the relentlessly blurring lines between journalism and commercial entertainment. Searing accounts of the breakdown in news reporting from Iraq, by Farnaz Fassihi and Michael Massing, amount to a case study in the weakness of the press at a time of war. Last but not least, in a coda to this volume, George Soros lays out a philosophical reckoning with the fact that open societies, like the United States, are no less susceptible to manipulation than are closed ones. Rather than resigning ourselves to this state of affairs, he concludes, we need to sharpen our defenses against manipulative rhetoric.

THIS COMPILATION predates the 2008 elections by exactly one year and the presidential contest forms its obvious backdrop. Critics will no doubt observe that the essayists are known for their progressive outlook. Yet their concerns rise above specific parties or ideological camps. Only a fool could assume that disingenuousness will magically vanish once a new occupant moves into the White House. Past occupants have done their bit to erect smoke screens around contentious policies, and so will future ones. The point of this book is to urge politicians on all sides to keep their words tethered to facts. It is an invitation to speak clearly and act honestly. And it is a reminder to the press, and to students of journalism, that keeping politics clean is a tough job. It is the daily task of reporters and editors to disenthrall public debate from bias, hyperbole, bombast, and lies.

Despite the maladies catalogued on these pages, the existence of this book is proof enough that for Americans, Orwell's worst fears remain safely consigned to literature—scary, perhaps, but hard to confuse with our present reality. What Orwell knew well was the threat of Totalitarianism: the horror of Fascism and the creeping shadow of Communism. What he didn't know—what he couldn't really know—was how modern consumer society would mold propaganda to its own form. Contemporary methods of persuasion are subtle, insidious, sugarcoated, focus-grouped, and market-tested—and comparable in their effectiveness to anything served up by despots and demagogues of the past. Today's political messages are distilled in the laboratories of public relations and consumer branding to achieve maximum potency. Their power to shape emotions and opinions lies in their uncanny ability to get under people's skin without arousing in citizens a powerful immune reaction. If Big Brother had had these tools, he'd still be around.

As it happens, I am one of the few contributors to this book who has lived under an "Orwellian" state, albeit a fairly toothless one. I grew up in Hungary in the twilight years of one-party rule—what Communist propagandists liked to call "existing socialism"—under a brand of Totalitarianism that was hardly total. Most people in "existing socialism" didn't internalize its simpleminded ideology. The situation was markedly different in the heyday of Nazi and Communist repression, and, as the next essay reminds us, in countries such as China, which succeeded in implementing a more creative and culturally embedded language of mind control. But in an Eastern Europe disenchanted by the tragedies of 1956 and 1968, we could clearly tell who was "us" and who was "them." Our hearts and minds were already warming to Western pop culture. Party propaganda, however stifling, was a relic from the Stone Age of communication. It had all the subtlety of a megaphone blasting workers' songs from a lamppost.

Around the year 1978, my schoolmates and I were sent to the annual May Day parade. As a special honor, we were asked to be part of a living tableau, a form of Communist pageantry that is nowadays practiced mainly in North Korea. It consists of hundreds of children holding up flags, like human Benday dots, to spell out slogans like "The friendship between socialist brother nations is everlasting." On the big day, we showed up in our uniforms, flags at the ready. We prepared to march in front of a marble tribune lined with waving Party dignitaries. Just as we embarked on our procession, heavy rainfall exploded from the sky. And we quickly discovered that the organizers had neglected to prepare for this meteorological intervention. The fabric dye in our flags was bleeding profusely. Green, blue, and crimson ink stained our hands and faces. Our human poster was dissolving.

Only a decade would pass before the Iron Curtain fell, taking down a vast internally consistent apparatus of ideological control. But there is a deeper lesson to this story. The flaw in our May Day tableau lay not in its execution, but in its guiding premise. Even if it hadn't been raining, our slogans could only have been read by the politicians standing above our heads. The people parading in front of them—the putative targets of state propaganda—couldn't see a thing.

Totalitarian propaganda, the sort Orwell mused about in *1984*, serves mainly to reassure the rulers, not to win over the ruled. Contemporary political communication—the kind Orwell presaged in "Politics and the English Language" but never saw fully formed—works in the reverse. It is trained at the end user. It insinuates itself into language, speech, and patterns of culture. Its goal is not to command people to act, but to seduce them. It functions not through external pressure, but through internalized belief. It's how we get things done in an advanced free-market democracy. And it is the form of deception that citizens of open societies need to worry about the most.

*   *   *

As THIS BOOK'S EDITOR, I would like to thank, above all, the contributors for writing original essays on short notice, and PublicAffairs for embracing the project under a tight deadline. Morgen Van Vorst provided expert editorial input and Becky Schutt advanced the behind-the-scenes logistics. This project would not have come about without the generous support of the Open Society Institute and its staff and the originating joint initiative of the Annenberg School for Communication at the University of Southern California, the Graduate School of Journalism at Columbia University, the Graduate School of Journalism at the University of California at Berkeley, the Joan Shorenstein Center on the Press, Politics and Public Policy at Harvard University, and the Medill School of Journalism at Northwestern University. Current and former deans of the schools at Berkeley, Columbia, and USC Annenberg helped to guide the project to its present form and contributed essays to this anthology. I am personally grateful to my friend Orville Schell, whose introduction follows, for inviting me to participate.

—August 2007

Follies of Orthodoxy

ORVILLE SCHELL

*He is unique in being immensely serious, and in
connecting good prose with liberty . . . [and in
believing that] if we write and speak clearly, we are
likely to think clearly and to remain comparatively free.*

—E. M. Forster on George Orwell[1]

George Orwell, who did so much to call attention to the ways in which the totalitarian movements of the last century corrupted political life, understood almost intuitively how propaganda was fundamental in their success. Drawing on his experiences with Fascism in the Spanish Civil War and his knowledge of Russian Communism, he examined how, by controlling language and discourse, and through the relentless repetition of half-truths and lies, official propaganda could sway and control the thinking of ordinary people (often with such finesse that many never comprehended the full measure of their actual compromise).

In "Politics and the English Language" (1946), perhaps his most influential essay, Orwell held language out as a critical "instrument for expressing rather than for concealing or preventing thought."[2] By pointing out the increasingly complex ways in which corrupted language precipitates chains of cause and effect that lead to corrupted thinking and distorted politics, his essay has become one of our most durable literary monuments on language and propaganda. (The term *propaganda* was born in the Papacy in 1622 when Pope Gregory XV established a committee of cardinals, called the *Congregatio de Propaganda Fide*, or Congregation for Propagating the Faith. This clerical body was established much as Departments of Propaganda were later established by Communist parties, namely, to create orthodoxy by making sure that priests were properly inoculated with canonic doctrine before being dispatched on evangelistic missions abroad.)

As in Catholicism, where the wrong use of words could bring charges of apostasy and where the Church tried to control what was said and written in order to circumscribe free-thinking, Orwell worried over the political effects of governmental control of language.

"A man may take a drink because he feels himself to be a failure, and then fail all the more completely because he drinks," he wrote. "It is the same thing that is happening with the English language. If one gets rid of these habits one can think more clearly, and to think clearly is a necessary first step towards political regeneration. . . . Above all what is needed is to let the meaning choose the word, and not the other way around."[3]

Repeatedly, Orwell returned in his writing to this idea that a state of health in a body politic is dependent on a careful and deliberate use of language. Newspeak, used by state propagandists in Orwell's famous futuristic novel *1984,* was effective, in Orwell's view, because it had "the power" to render people incapable of "grasping analogies, of failing to perceive logical errors, of misunderstanding the simplest argument, if they are inimical to Ingsoc [the official ideology], and of being bored or repelled by any train of thought which is capable of leading in a heretical direction."

But, what offended Orwell most about this kind of propaganda was that it engenders a "protective stupidity."[4]

In *1984,* one of Orwell's own fictional characters—his Trotsky-like Newspeak-doublespeak ideologue "Goldstein"— observes, "By comparison with that existing today, all the tyrannies of the past were half-hearted and inefficient."[5]

If Orwell were to return to our post-1984 world, it would be interesting to know what he might make of the situation. For, as horrified as he was during the middle of the last century by what he saw of propaganda's capacity to distort and corrupt, he nonetheless retained naïve optimism in the inviolability of the individual soul, where, he liked to imagine, human qualities such as love, loyalty, and devotion might still find refuge. Indeed, he almost quaintly believed that though "they" could control everything around one in the external world, "They can't get inside you."[6]

So, despite his rather gloomy prognosis about the powers of Totalitarianism and propaganda, Orwell harbored a somewhat innocent belief that there were nonetheless aspects of a human individual still not fully accessible to propaganda's predations.

In *1984,* his hero, Winston, proclaims that "[t]hey could lay bare in the utmost detail everything that you had done or said or thought; but the inner heart, whose workings were mysterious even to yourself, remained impregnable."[7]

What Orwell could not know in the 1930s and 1940s was that Totalitarianism and its propaganda apparatus would ultimately succeed in penetrating "the inner heart" of individuals. Nor could he have known how much more sophisticated and persuasive propaganda was still destined to become, how in the latter part of the twentieth century latter-day avatars would graft onto this already dark art a whole host of new and extremely powerful elements. In fact, what was in Orwell's time already a frighteningly manipulative tool would over the next few decades take several more quantum leaps forward in its ability to subliminally deceive and influence. It did so by evolving in a Darwinian manner, by confronting the challenges of capitalism and democracy, and then under the pressure of this natural selection, mutating to incorporate traits from each as if it were cloning new genetic material onto its figurative genome. It was in this manner that propaganda's genetic makeup gained a new hybrid vigor, achieving an unforeseen level of sophistication and efficaciousness that would doubtless have astounded Orwell. In this process, there were several major evolutionary breakthroughs worthy of note.

The first came about as China imported Stalin's form of Marxist-Leninist propaganda and imbued it with "Chinese characteristics," turning it into "Mao Zedong Thought."

The second significant evolutionary step occurred because of explicit advances in the burgeoning world of psychoanalytical thought. A new approach, pioneered by Sigmund Freud, plumbed the depths of human unconsciousness to form a revolutionary corpus of systematized theories on how to understand, and even heal, the inner workings of the human psyche. Through a quite unholy matrimonial convergence, "old-style" political propaganda became fortified by Freudian insights about human insecurity, weakness, yearning, and guilt. The result: new forms of manipulation in which overt political coercion merged with an array of subtle but powerful covert psychological mechanisms.

One of the pioneers of some of these new psychological mechanisms was Edward Bernays, the father of "public relations," who also happened to be Sigmund Freud's nephew, a fact that conveniently allowed him to borrow some of his famous uncle's understandings about human psychology in order to write a figurative textbook on how to induce people to buy more consumer goods.

"If we understand the mechanisms and motives of the group mind," Bernays presciently observed, "is it not possible to control and regiment the masses according to our will without their knowing it? The recent practice of propaganda has proved that is possible."[8]

In this brave new world of "mass persuasion," Bernays hoped to use innovative advertising to wean consumers away from what he called a "needs-based" culture toward one that was "desire-based." As his business partner, Paul Mazur, succinctly put it, "We must shape a new mentality. Man's desires must overshadow his needs."[9] And if there was one thing Bernays's eminent uncle understood, it was how important people's unconscious desires are in forming whom they become, how they develop, and what they want to consume.

When public relations theory and its application to commercial advertising—which Orwell had derided as "the rattling of a stick inside a swill bucket"[10]—became available to authoritarian regimes as a means to bolster their own propaganda and control efforts, a new industrial-strength brew that was infinitely more subtle and convincing than anything that had preceded it was born. Its power lay in its capacity to sway people into either passively accepting whatever version of reality "the powers that be" wished them to accept or making them want things that were manifestly illogical or antithetical to their interests. The most impressive feature of this second evolutionary stage in propaganda's historical progress was that although it had originally evolved as a form of "selling" goods and services, it soon migrated to politics. Here it took root not only in capitalist societies but also in societies labeled "socialist," or "revolutionary."

The third, and last, evolutionary development in propaganda was brought about by the development of technology, particularly in the electronic media. What could be achieved visually on television (and later on the Internet) was far higher on the periodic table of persuasiveness than anything that had preceded it. This new medium was capable of making almost any message seductive and convincing. Even in the most pluralistic, diverse societies with decades of dedication to a free press, television soon managed to create such powerful images and such a forceful one-way conversation that there was little room for the kind of interactive discourse imagined by the architects of modern democracies, such as Enlightenment thinkers in Europe and the founding fathers in the United States. When crossbred with forms of twentieth-century totalitarian ideology and propaganda, television became a powerful new form of indoctrination for both commercial and political purposes.

It was the Chinese Communist Revolution, heir to both Confucianism and Marxism-Leninism—two political cultures not known for their interest in the interior psychological worlds on which Freud and Bernays had focused—that paradoxically contributed a new dimension of psychic persuasion to the dynamics of propaganda as inherited from the Union of Soviet Socialist Republics (USSR). Much of propaganda's power derived from a cryptic amalgamation of Leninism and Confucianism, or perhaps it would be more accurate to say from some of the psychological mechanisms that were deeply rooted within China's traditional cultural soul by Confucianism, which became conjoined with Leninism.

It was ironic that Mao's new socialist revolution should have ended up relying, albeit somewhat surreptitiously, on Confucian tradition and its inner imperatives toward conformity as a form of psychological control, at the same time that propagandists were also decrying Confucian culture as "backward," "oppressive," and "feudal." But by allying the coercive power of Soviet-style propaganda with this underground reservoir of Chinese tradition, the Party accomplished a far more effective system of political control than Stalin had managed to achieve in Russia.

At the heart of the Leninist system that molted into its Maoist incarnation was the fundamental Confucian notion that personal "self-cultivation" and "self-study" are the path not only to becoming a *junzi* ("a gentleman," or an "exemplary person") but also to restoring order in society. In the Confucian scheme of things, one that had several millennia of practice in China, the source of almost any problem was understood to lay in the self. Thus, the primary locus of remedy was usually perceived as beginning with the self through a process of "self-cultivation" and eventual "rectification."

As *Daxue* ("The Great Learning")—the second Confucian classic of *Sishu* ("The Four Books")—puts it: "From the Son of heaven on down to the common people, all must regard cultivation of the personal life as the root or foundation. There is never a case where the root is in disorder and yet the branches are in order."[11]

In other words, Chinese were taught traditionally that through "self-cultivation" one might "rectify" not only his own individual thoughts and mind to become a better person, but also that he might also play his proscribed part in bringing about "harmony" in human relations, the state, and the larger world.

The Chinese personality therefore contained a deeply ingrained tendency to believe that all disorder "under heaven," *tianxia,* grows out of a failure of the individual to adequately cultivate the self. This mindset provided a huge portal through which the Chinese Communist Party could drive its new Leninist version of revolution, which also emphasized self-reformation as a key element in "making revolution." The process of undergoing "ideological study," "criticism and self-criticism," and then finally making a confession of error as a "correct" pathway to political rebirth lay at the heart of the Maoist vision of how individuals could be politically remolded into revolutionary "comrades" and how China could be transformed into a socialist society.

In the myriad mass political campaigns that he launched, Mao relied on the almost autonomic response among Chinese when criticized to turn inward to introspection, self-cultivation, and confession, rather than to outward remonstration, as the proper course of action for becoming realigned with family, clan, society, or body politic.

As Mao wrote in his 1945 essay "On Coalition Government," the "conscientious practice of self-criticism is still another hallmark distinguishing our Party from all other political parties. As we say, dust will accumulate if a room is not cleaned regularly, our faces will get dirty if not washed regularly. Our comrades' minds and our Party's work may also collect dust, and also need sweeping and washing. . . . Fear neither criticism nor self-criticism, and apply such good popular Chinese maxims as, 'Say all you know and say it without reserve.'"[12]

Although his school of traditional political philosophy was later savagely attacked during the Cultural Revolution in the Communist propaganda classic *How to Be a Good Communist*, former People's Republic of China president Liu Shaoqi nonetheless himself quoted Confucius to admonish aspiring Communist Party members to cultivate "an ear that is an obedient organ for the reception of truth."[13]

In this case, Party members were not seeking to become *junzi* but to remove bourgeois taint or insinuations of "counterrevolutionary" backgrounds or activities and "remold" their thoughts and themselves in order to become better revolutionaries.

Westerners have tended to view this elaborate process as Party-instigated "brainwashing," a charge that was not entirely inaccurate. But what the West tended to miss about this interesting new psycho-political remolding process was that once catalyzed by the Party, much of the process of reorientation was taken over by the victim himself to become self-initiated. The Chinese Communist Party had perfected an extremely effective regimen of thought reform that combined the new command authoritarianism of Lenin with the older, deeply ingrained traditional authoritarianism of Confucius that called on Chinese to reform themselves. Both relied on the study of official texts and then on a process of cultivation to instill orthodox belief, as well as obedience to leadership, all of which were understood as the necessary preconditions for being viewed as a worthwhile human being as well as for maintaining social order.

As the psychiatrist Robert J. Lifton wrote in his classic study, "Thought Reform and the Psychology of Totalism," "Confucianism shares with Communism the assumption that men can and should remake themselves, first as a process of changing their environment, and then as a means of adapting themselves to that environment."[14]

In both the Confucian and the Maoist worldview there is a presupposition that engaging in personal, moralistic self-education is every human being's obligation to both themselves and to society. This sense of responsibility to remold oneself to fit into the social group bred an almost innate yearning to fulfill prescribed obligations to family, society, and the state. It also created a profound sense of disease for individuals who found themselves in a state of social or political ostracism. It is perhaps for this reason that the term "political dissident" has had such a negative connotation for most Chinese. In any event, it was this tendency that enabled the Chinese Communist Party to quickly ensnare whomever it chose to accuse of political incorrectness in a masterful web of self-incrimination and often even psychological self-immolation.

Lifton described such a situation as engendering an ethos of extreme psychological pressure to reform oneself so that accused individuals end up feeling "an irresistible demand for an admission of guilt" as the only imaginable way to purge themselves of the burden of accusation. This is why confessing in China came to be so common that even Deng Xiaoping famously wrote an abjectly self-abnegating confession during the Cultural Revolution.

The Party seemed to understand that if political control was the goal, it was far more effective to get people to control themselves than to use external coercion. The transference of blame for an accusation from the accuser to the accused was indeed a masterful sleight of hand. The process fed on what the Chinese intellectual historian Sun Longji called "the disorganization of the self," which results when a victim's individual rights are abrogated so totally that all power of resistance is lost, and the individual becomes willing to join his accusers in attacking *himself* in a desperate effort toward rehabilitation. After all, in such a situation where the Chinese Communist Revolution and the Party were deemed infallible, what conclusion was available to an accused other than: "It must be me who is at fault."

In this neat conspiracy of Leninist politics and Confucian psychology, external accusation was fortified by self-blame and finally even a yearning for judgment and punishment as the only imaginable pathway for the remission of sins. Happily for the Party, many victims of this process ended up not needing to be sentenced or imprisoned at all; once caught in this web, they became so psychologically immobilized with a deep sense of their own failure to reform that they were no longer politically threatening.

By going back to the future and updating Russian propaganda techniques with aspects of Chinese tradition, the Party had stumbled upon an extraordinarily powerful new tool. I say "stumbled upon" because I have yet to see any Chinese Communist Party tract that fully analyzes, or even partially understands, the magnitude of this seemingly inadvertent discovery. In fact, for a more complete understanding of this elusive psychological process, we need to turn beyond China to Western literature.

The Czech writer Milan Kundera is perhaps the most insightful analyst of this complex and subtle psycho-political process. Kundera, who understood something of Communist propaganda himself from his experience in Czechoslovakia, referred to this process as an "auto-culpabilization machine,"[15] a form of political control that the literary works of Franz Kafka (the master of guilt in the human psyche) and Fyodor Dostoyevsky (who knew a thing or two about crime and punishment himself) can help illuminate.

In the example of Raskolnikov, the hero of Dostoyevsky's *Crime and Punishment*, Kundera explained that as readers, we are met with "the well-known situation where *the offense seeks punishment.*" But Kundera observed that in *The Trial*, perhaps Franz Kafka's greatest work, "the logic is reversed. The punished person does not know the reason for the punishment. The absurdity of the punishment is so unbearable that to find peace, the accused needs to find justification for his penalty; *the punishment seeks the offense.* [In fact,] in this pseudo-psychological world, *the punished beg for recognition of their guilt.*"[16]

How could victims, who have themselves been so wronged, become so complicit in their own incrimination, punishment, and downfall? Through the expectation that "criticism and self-criticism" would right the balance, the Chinese Communist Party managed to initiate a process that finally drew victims into psychological prosecution of themselves.

With incredible lucidity, Kundera described how this process worked on well-meaning people, especially those who aspired to be good, i.e., loyal revolutionaries and Party stalwarts:

"All their lives they had entirely identified themselves with the Party," he wrote. "When suddenly it became their prosecutor, they agreed like Joseph K [the anti-hero in Kafka's *The Trial*], 'to examine their whole lives, their entire pasts, down to the last details' to find the hidden offense, and, in the end, to confess to imaginary crimes."[17]

Since all accused people yearn for the succor of absolution, the most comforting place to affix guilt is not on some exogenous accuser, court, or tribunal that is uncontrollable, but on themselves. Why? Because at least here, individuals can imagine that they have the power to expunge whatever crime they have been accused of through self-examination and confession, processes that they do control. That was the implicit bargain that the Party seemed to offer.

So, though it may seem odd to explain how the Chinese Communist Party succeeded in enhancing the potency of propaganda and thought control by citing Western writers, the truth is that neither Confucian scholars nor Marxist-Leninist theorists were part of particularly inward-looking cultures that were fully cognizant of the inner workings of the system of control they had accidentally developed. After all, Freudian psychological theory never gained much purchase in China during either the traditional or revolutionary periods. And thus it is, indeed, something of an irony that the Chinese, especially Marxists, should have perfected a system that involved such complex and subtle forms of psychological intrusion and control.

This was the brilliance—if one can use such a word in such a brutal instance—of China's evolutionarily improved form of propaganda that, in the end, made even the USSR's efforts look rather old-fashioned. Lifton goes so far as to describe what China achieved as "the modern totalitarian expression of a national genius."[18]

Whether what they accomplished really constitutes "genius" is difficult to say. But what can be said with certitude is that the Chinese Communist regimen of propaganda and thought control certainly was effective in defoliating China of liberal traditions and thought.

"Every line of serious work I have written since 1936 has been written, directly or indirectly, *against* totalitarianism and *for* democratic socialism, as I understand it," wrote Orwell in "Why I Write." It is more than a little interesting to wonder how he might want to update his thinking from the vantage point of the twenty-first century.

China's "contribution" to the development of propaganda is only one link in a long chain of evolution. Indeed, this evolutionary course continues in its cryptic progress to create ever more inventive forms of beguilement. Right here in America, subtler, slicker, and increasingly toxic traits are being annealed onto propaganda through an ongoing process that now continues to crossbreed, this time miscegenating not Confucianism and Leninism but politics, psychology, and commercial advertising. The result is that the kind of open and truthful political discourse so esteemed by George Orwell is being distorted in increasingly alarming ways, putting our vaunted notion of a "free press," so eloquently delineated by our founding fathers, in greater and greater peril. Indeed, we may be arriving at something of a tipping-point moment for American democracy, one where the admonitions of the likes of George Orwell and George Washington seem at once profound and quaint.

"If men are to be precluded from offering their sentiments on a matter which may involve the most serious and alarming consequences that can invite the consideration of mankind," wrote the first president, "reason is of no use for us; the freedom of speech may be taken away, and dumb and silent we may be led, like sheep to the slaughter."[19]

The chapters that you are about to read in this book will, we hope, help update the investigation that was begun by George Orwell half a century ago. It is also, alas, probably safe to assume that propaganda's evolution has hardly run its course.

PART ONE

Language and Politics

Orwell Then and Now

DAVID RIEFF

Writers write for all sorts of reasons—some generic, some idiosyncratic. From the belief that one has something to say, to the drive to have others pay attention to what one has to say (anything but the same thing), to an incapacity to do anything else, rationales abound. But by no means the least of them is the idea of writing as conferring a species of immortality. One will become dust, but one's works will endure—intellectual and artistic DNA that does not disappear with one's last breath but rather lives on for a very long time.

Of course, the odds of a writer being remembered for very many years, let alone a century or centuries, after his or her death are slim. For every Sophocles there are a thousand Elinor Glyns; for every Shakespeare, innumerable G. A. Hentys and Leon Urises, to name two writers vastly celebrated in their respective eras and either now already forgotten or at least heading that way at Mach 2.

It is true that works no longer read for pleasure are often of value to scholars. One can go further and say that bad novels expressing the conventional sentiments of their time, and trite essays expressing its conventional wisdom, are often of greater value to the historian than great works that, if not timeless exactly, certainly are great in some measure because they largely transcend their era and their authors' prejudices. This is probably clearer in painting than in literature (we do not much care that much of Rubens's best work was propaganda for the Stuart kings). But one can be moved by Dickens without sharing the sentimental English mercantilist liberalism so central to the denouements of many of his best books or swept up by the genius of Dostoyevsky without accepting for an instant the Christian subservience to authority that is one of its deepest messages.

At least for those who love them, though, fiction and poetry are a continuum across the centuries. In creative writing, there is nothing odd about preferring the past to the present—choosing, say, Laurence Sterne over Thomas Pynchon, or Edith Wharton over John Updike. But even the best nonfiction tends to date quickly, particularly when it is frankly political and anchored in the controversies of its day. Randolph Bourne was a great soul and much he had to say about early twentieth-century America was of great importance. But largely speaking, one reads him when one is trying to understand that period in U.S. history. Most often, it is only when the essayist has exceptional literary merit as well as a way with arguments that posterity is long interested. Cyril Connolly was a wonderful stylist and his work may endure a long time. In contrast, the American critic Irving Howe had a wonderful mind and was right on most of the issues of his time (far righter than Connolly), but it is hard to imagine him being read a century on.

For all the ways in which the self-loving adage that writers are the unacknowledged legislators of mankind has been assimilated into the common wisdom of the age (and what a firm grip the Romantics still have on our collective throat!), very few writers are treated that way in their own lifetimes and almost none for very long after they have died. But once in a great while, however, one encounters a writer who seems not only to have a finger on the pulse of his or her own era, but also to have something authoritative to say to posterity. Dr. Johnson was preeminent in this role for much of the nineteenth century. Since his death in 1950 at the age of forty-six, it has fallen to George Orwell.

Whether Orwell himself would have relished being treated simultaneously as seer, secular saint, yardstick of conscience, and arbiter of political good sense is surely doubtful. He was not without vanity, but he was both too much of a natural contrarian and too skeptical of human motives to have taken such adulation at face value. Like Simone Weil, whom he would have loathed (a dislike Weil would have reciprocated with interest), Orwell had an almost pitch-perfect talent for making things as difficult for himself as possible and a penitent's tropism toward physical discomfort and privation even when there were easier and more comfortable roads open to him. Weil for all intents and purposes ensured her own death when, gravely ill, she insisted on subsisting on the official ration for people in Nazi-occupied France even though virtually everybody in France at the time had extra sources of food. Orwell, his tuberculosis worsening, left London where he might have been properly looked after for the cold isolation of the Isle of Jura off western Scotland, where he tried to write, make furniture, and raise pigs as his health went from bad to worse.

Both Weil and Orwell were "judgers." Their standards were high, and their opinions severe. Few people measured up, perhaps least of all those with whom they shared important political and cultural affinities. Weil was at war with her own Jewish background and with her Catholic faith. Orwell, as the political historian George Lichtheim, who knew him, once told me, seemed puzzled at how he had wound up with so many Jews and homosexuals for comrades, and in many ways was as sentimental about England—or at least a certain fantasy image of England—as any of his more conventional classmates at Eton or colleagues in the Burmese colonial police. Unable to praise liberally, it is hard to imagine Orwell accepting the Niagaras of praise that have poured over him since his death.

Would the writer whose stock-in-trade was the telling of unpleasant truths—truths to power on behalf of the powerless, but also truths about power to people whom Orwell felt criticized it without understanding it—have really reveled in what has now been almost sixty years of encomia? He was not without ego, so perhaps he would have succumbed—at least for a time. But I find it hard to believe that, in the end, Orwell's natural cussedness would not eventually have reasserted itself and that he would not have wondered what all the fuss about himself was finally all about?

And the praise has been as curious as it has been lavish. Most influential writers are "claimed" by one political side both in their own time and after their deaths. In Orwell's time, it was clear that Eliot was a man of the right and Auden of the left, and apart from the fact that Auden's leftism seems increasingly marginal in terms of his work and opinions, this judgment has endured. In contrast, Orwell is a writer who always insisted that he was a man of the left, and yet he is now claimed by both the left (apart from an extreme fringe for whom Orwell's anti-communism remains anathema) and the right. The neoconservative writer Norman Podhoretz once wrote an essay on Orwell insisting that were he alive today, he too would be a neoconservative. At the same time, Orwell is routinely invoked in descriptions of the current political depredations of the American right (a claim exemplified by this volume).

Weighing these mutually excluding acts of appropriation, it is hard not to feel that the actual George Orwell disappears the more the debate intensifies. It is as if he had become a kind of Rorschach blot onto which contestants in our contemporary political controversies can project their own opinions, but using Orwell as nineteenth-century politicians used the Bible—as debate-settling textual authority. Opponents of George Bush think that Orwell would have seen in the Karl Rove propaganda machine the realization of his fears of political "Newspeak." Supporters of the Iraq war insist that Orwell was first and foremost an anti-totalitarian and thus would have welcomed the overthrow of so vicious a tyrant as Saddam Hussein. For the right, campus political correctness is totalitarian. For the left, it is Orwell's fear of a controlled media that resonates today in this period of increasing media monopoly and capitalist political consensus.

The truth is that none of the people who have expressed themselves so recklessly and self-servingly about what Orwell would have thought and where he would have stood have the right to opine believably about either. To state the obvious: Orwell died fifty-seven years ago, when the Cold War was in its infancy, the European colonial empires still existed, the global predominance of the United States was not clear (to Orwell at least), globalization and the information economy did not exist, the mass migration of the people of the Global South to the rich world had not yet begun, feminism had not yet transformed the family, and neither the Internet nor the biological revolution had taken place. To claim that one can deduce from what Orwell said and what one believes he stood for in his own time what he would have thought of the early twenty-first century is either a vulgar quest for an authority to ratify one's own views, a fantasy about the transferability of the past to the present (itself a kind of narcissistic rejection of the past's authenticity), or both. We haven't a clue what Orwell would have thought or what side he would have taken. Nor should we have.

What we do have the right to is the claim that posterity can always make on the work of a great writer like George Orwell. We can say that Orwell's work, whether it be the description of Communism in *Animal Farm* and *Homage to Catalonia*, of Totalitarianism in *1984*, or of the poor in *Down and Out in Paris and London* and *The Road to Wigan Pier*, and in his essential essays on the relationship between language and politics, is a profound inspiration to us—not a shortcut to making the points we deem important, but an example to be emulated of how to think and how to write. To claim more for Orwell is not to honor him but to deny his work its specific gravity. He is a writer, not a guide.

And surely that should be enough.

The Limits of Language

Nicholas Lemann

C an there be a political writer who has not fallen in love with George Orwell's 1946 essay, "Politics and the English Language"? Part of its appeal is what's appealing about all of Orwell—its directness and honesty, its plainspokenness, its faith, against all evidence, that human affairs can be conducted morally, its sense of being on the side of ordinary people, not of the sophisticated and powerful. The only people Orwell attacks by name in "Politics and the English Language" are two celebrated academics, Harold Laski and Lancelot Hogben, not the kind of minor-grade politicians and bureaucrats who would have made easy targets.

"Politics and the English Language" begins as a lesson, and quite a good one, in how to write well (delivered in the form of an attack on people who write badly), and ends with the hope that better writing can engender a better society. What idea could be more attractive to writers than that what we do, if improved along the lines Orwell suggests, can improve not just our readers' experience of our work, but the lives of everybody?

To Orwell, the connection between the English language and politics was that the debasement of the latter requires the corruption of the former. "In our age," he wrote—meaning, the age of the rise of Totalitarianism—"there is no such thing as 'keeping out of politics.' All issues are political issues, and politics itself is a mass of lies, evasions, folly, hatred and schizophrenia. When the general atmosphere is bad, language must suffer." But saying this generates the hope—highly qualified, as hope always was in Orwell's work—that better, clearer language could rob bad politics of its voice, and thereby might bring it to an end.

Orwell began work on his masterpiece, *1984*, not long after "Politics and the English Language" was published (the essay owes some of its resonance to the way it foreshadows Newspeak, the great literary device Orwell invented for the novel). Although "Politics and the English Language" is probably the best known of all Orwell's essays, at the time he wrote it—for *Horizon,* a magazine edited by his old schoolmate Cyril Connolly—he was an extremely busy freelancer. It was one of more than 100 pieces Orwell published in 1946. Even as it advocates care and precision in the use of language, it is more passionate than systematic.

To produce *1984*, on the other hand, Orwell, by then a dying man, removed himself to a location about as far from the setting of the book as one can imagine: a house on the sea, at the end of miles of unpaved road, on the remote Scottish island of Jura. Newspeak is a fully worked-out system far more horrifying than the examples Orwell gives us in "Politics and the English Language." Its aim is to make individual independent thought impossible, by depriving the mind of the words necessary to form ideas other than those fed to it by the state. Newspeak at once radically limits and shortens the number of words available to people (so that everyone has to operate at the linguistic level of a three- or four-year-old) and turns all words denoting concepts into long, incomprehensible, bureaucratized euphemisms, devoid of meaning and unable to provoke debate or resistance. Take away words, and you have taken away mental function; take away mental function, and you have taken away the possibility of political action.

Because Newspeak is an aspect of a fully realized work of art, it has the quality of seamless self-contained perfection that art often has: It exists literarily on terms that make it powerful and inarguable. "Politics and the English Language," because it is farther from perfection, is more interesting to think about today. Its conceptual roughness makes possible a real consideration of Orwell's proposition that bad language always produces bad politics (and good language can produce good politics), in a way that Newspeak does not.

The primary villain in "Politics and the English Language" is the kind of fancy, pretentious, imprecise prose that is usually purveyed by intellectuals (Orwell's particular targets were intellectuals on the left), not the state. Nobody who has read the essay can ever use a formulation such as "not unlike" again with a clear conscience. Throughout the essay, Orwell wanders into what seems to be a blanket condemnation of all use of abstractions in political discussion. Life without "democracy," "justice," "science," "class," and "equality" is a lot more difficult to contemplate happily than life without "not unlike"—these are not, after all, terms purposely made incomprehensible in the manner of Newspeak. Although Orwell's language is wonderfully clear, his thought, on this crucial point, is not. Sometimes he seems to be saying that his despair about virtually all political discussion is an artifact of a bad historical moment—which would mean there is hope. But in concluding, he wrote, "Political language

. . . is designed to make lies sound truthful and murder respectable, and to give an appearance of solidity to pure wind." That sounds pretty hopeless. Orwell is so uncomfortable with big, complex societies that it's hard to tell whether he would ever approve of political writing that seeks to make conceptual, rather than concrete and specific, observations.

Bad writing is, unfortunately, eternal; surely there is even more of it today, by weight, than there was in 1946. As a writing guide, "Politics and the English Language" is, more than sixty years after publication, absolutely useful. Whether Orwell's idea—that better writing, and clearer language, can actually improve politics—applies today is a tougher question.

There are really two distinct kinds of bad political writing: the overcomplicated, unclear kind; and propaganda. The first kind is dangerous because people in power can use it to fuzz up what they are doing and thus avoid accountability—think of a word like *renditions*—but it is usually not persuasive, because persuasion is not its intent. Propaganda, on the other hand, is often quite beautifully and clearly written. When it works, it works by virtue of being simple and memorable. What is dangerous about propaganda is that it is misleading, but its success seems to disprove Orwell's implication that all bad ideas must be clumsily expressed. Consider the following extract from President Bush's speech to a joint session of Congress on September 20, 2001, in which he unveiled the "War on Terror":

On September the 11th, enemies of freedom committed an act of war against our country. Americans have known wars—but for the past 136 years, they have been wars on foreign soil, except for one Sunday in 1941. Americans have known the casualties of war—but not at the center of a great city on a peaceful morning. Americans have known surprise attacks—but never before on thousands of civilians. All of this was brought upon us in a single day—and night fell on a different world, a world where freedom itself is under attack.

This would strike many people today as practically the locus classicus—as Orwell surely would not have put it—of the kind of language we call "Orwellian." (At the time, it struck almost nobody that way.) Bush was responding to a successful terrorist attack by declaring war, not against the attackers themselves but against unspecified "enemies of freedom." Thus, as in *1984*, the United States was in a war without a definite beginning or end point, against whomever Bush wanted it to be against. Still, the speech wasn't exactly Newspeak—its rhetoric was neither purposely obscure nor flat and simple to the point of meaninglessness. It was meant to have a genuine, persuasive emotional effect, and it did. Neither, except in its violation of Orwell's proposed ban on the word *freedom*, is it representative of the kind of rhetoric "Politics and the English Language" was aimed against. It was vivid and (to quote Orwell) "all its words are those of everyday life." The one exemplar of good writing Orwell singled out for praise in "Politics and the English Language" was the King James version of the Bible—a text that Bush and his speechwriter at the time, Michael Gerson, obviously also admired and tried to use as a model. The challenge that "Politics and the English Language" puts before us today is in determining how far we can get politically through linguistic reform.

All politicians use slogans. Most significant legislation is given a meaning-obscuring name, for instance, the USA PATRIOT Act and the No Child Left Behind Act. The way we respond to these uses of language is partly conditioned by our political preferences. Conservatives, who admire Orwell today no less than liberals do, find Franklin Roosevelt's New Deal and Lyndon Johnson's Great Society (pretty names for great expansions in the charter of the federal welfare state) to be Orwellian uses of language. Every recent president has seemed to his opposition to have used political spin at an unprecedented and alarming level, and every party out of power believes that if it can only use language more effectively (as opposed to more honestly), it will win again. Is there a set of rules we can propose for the honest use of political language that transcends ideology, and that would stand up to the often unlovely exigencies of campaigning and government in a free society?

There is nothing wrong with Orwell's advice in "Politics and the English Language": Simple is better than complicated, concrete is better than abstract, careful is better than sloppy, think before you write. The experience of the last few years would lead me to add that in political language, function is far preferable to emotion: The words used to denote something the government does should have to do with the activity itself, not the values it is meant to embody or the feelings it is meant to activate. The war in Iraq yes, Operation Enduring Freedom no.

But this would get us only part of the way. There are real limits to how what's wrong with politics can be fixed linguistically. Many people participate in politics through group membership, not through consuming messages delivered through the mass media. People in interest groups, whether they're environmentalists or beet farmers, usually come to politics with their minds already made up, or at least with a frame of reference so powerful (legal abortion is like the Holocaust) that it lies completely outside the bounds of the general public debate. They are not susceptible to persuasion, but that means they can't easily be misled or brainwashed, either. The target of political language is the marginal players, not the committed ones; conversely, active and widespread political participation decreases the importance of language, and thus, for good or ill, reduces the role of writers, intellectuals, and propagandists in the political system.

To my mind, an even more frightening political prospect than the corruption of language is the corruption of information. Language, especially in the age of the Internet, is accessible to everybody. Some users of language are more powerful than others, some are more honest than others, and some are more adept than others—but the various ways of speaking about politics can at least compete with each other in the public square, and we can at least hope that the more honest and clear ways will triumph in the end. Information, on the other hand, is much less generally accessible than words. When the process of determining whether the facts of a situation have been intentionally corrupted by people in power (whether, let's say, Saddam Hussein had the ability to produce nuclear weapons, or whether a new drug has harmful side effects), there often is no corrective mechanism at hand, as there is in cases of the intentional corruption of language. Intellectual honesty about the gathering and use of facts and data is a riskier and more precious part of a free society than is intellectual honesty in language. We ought to guard it with the same zeal that animates Orwell's work on political speech.

Words in a Time of War:
On Rhetoric, Truth, and Power

MARK DANNER

From the totalitarian point of view history is something
to be created rather than learned.

—George Orwell, 1946

1.

We pride ourselves in being realists first of all, and thus we know
well, or tell ourselves we do, that "the first casualty when war
comes is truth." Yet Senator Hiram Johnson's oft-quoted dictum
comes down to us from 1918, a more innocent time, when the
hopes for truth and transparency at the heart of the Progressive
Era were foundering on the rhetorical exigencies of the Great
War. What can this truism mean nine decades later, when applied to a war that is itself in large part a rhetorical creation, a war
unbounded by space or by time, unlimited in extent and metaphysical in ambition: a forever war launched against evil itself?

Such is the "War on Terror," declared in the wake of the attacks of September 11, 2001, and fought with passionate rhetorical intensity in the half dozen years since. The enemy in this war, the president told Congress and the nation a week after the planes struck, was "heir to all the murderous ideologies of the twentieth century . . . follow[ing] in the path of Fascism, and Nazism, and Totalitarianism" and such a terrible foe called for nothing less than a campaign to "rid this world of evil." Though for a time the war remained mostly "virtual," fought mostly "on the dark side," as Vice President Dick Cheney put it, by intelligence officers, special forces, and, in Afghanistan, a large helping of aerial bombardment, this largely virtual conflict shortly gave birth to a real war, the invasion and occupation of Iraq. The stubborn refusal of the Iraq war to conclude on schedule (Pentagon plans called for all but a few tens of thousands of Americans to be out of Iraq by September 2003) and thus supply the promised "shining example of democracy in the Middle East" in time for the 2004 elections resulted in its wholesale absorption, *faute de mieux,* into the virtual war. And so Iraq, the failed war, now became, as the self-described "wartime president" dubbed it in his reelection campaign, "the central front of the war on terror."

Virtual war begets real war. Failure subsumes real war to virtual. Thus did virtual War on Terror became real, an affair of tanks, weekly casualty counts, and an infinitely receding horizon. As I write, President Bush and the Republican candidates to succeed him, with a losing war on their hands and no place to put it, find themselves working tirelessly, unceasingly, to keep the real war safely sheltered under the virtual canopy of the War on Terror, declaring Iraq "the critical battle" in "the defining ideological struggle of our time," in which defeat will lead to "the terrorists following us home." The Democrats, meantime, struggle equally hard to drag it back out, branding the Iraq war not only a failure but, more seriously still, a "distraction" from "the real war"—by which they mean, to add another twist of paradox, none other than the War on Terror. More surprising, perhaps, than the fact that the struggle over the ontological character of these wars now comprises the central rhetorical battleground of American politics is our own decided lack of surprise, our ongoing willingness to listen seriously to such verbal shadow play. We have come far since Hiram Johnson's simple bromides about war and truth.

George Orwell, it is safe to say, would not have been surprised. It was Orwell, after all, who nearly six decades ago fathered the idea of virtual conflict, creating the perpetual world war between the superstates of Oceania, Eurasia, and Eastasia that forms the background to *1984*. That never-ending, shape-shifting struggle, it is well to remember, was nearly bloodless, a perpetual war that, "if we judge it by the standards of previous wars, is merely an imposture . . . like the battles between certain ruminant animals whose horns are set at such an angle that they are incapable of hurting one another. But though it is unreal it is not meaningless. . . . [I]t helps to preserve the special mental atmosphere that a hierarchical society needs."

The comparison, of course, must be inexact. Thousands have died in the War on Terror, and many thousands more in Iraq. These wars are only partly virtual, and it is no accident that the struggle over their reality has attained such a central place in our politics. What Orwell dramatizes is an ideal, the Platonic form of virtual war. What he describes for us—what we must learn from him today—is the power of virtual war to reduce and refine boulders of international armed conflict down to their most valuable *political* ore. In his conception the great grinding mechanism of modern industrial warfare is stripped of all its material attributes: armies, fighting, even death—all but "the special mental atmosphere" that wars produce. The glittering, priceless ore that remains is the politician's lodestone, for glowing at its heart is that most lucrative of political emotions: fear. War produces fear. But so also does the rhetoric of war. This— Orwell's precious insight—leads to the central lesson he brings us about our own perpetual war: What terrorists ultimately produce is not death or mayhem but fear; and in a War on Terror the rich political benefits of that most lucrative emotion will inevitably be shared—between the terrorists themselves and the political leaders who lead the fight against them.

2.

Perhaps it would have surprised Orwell, poet laureate of the Cold War, to find himself so much in our thoughts in this second decade of the post–Cold War age. The Soviet Union is fifteen years dead, its imperium in the East long since ended. China has entered into a peculiar economic symbiosis with the American capitalist juggernaut, fabricating most of its consumer goods and holding in payment most of its debt. And in this new post-ideological world no writer is more vital than George Orwell, not least because he helps us see how deeply that earlier struggle has marked us, helps us read the signs it has inscribed on the body of our politics.

Gazing at the solemn White House ceremony on December 14, 2004, watching in inarticulate wonder as the newly reelected president placed the Medal of Freedom around the necks of three high officials, I began to perceive, dancing deep in my memory, a line of Orwell's that I could not quite grasp. Before me on the television screen, neck bent for the president, stood General (ret.) Tommy Franks, who had led the initial "combat phase" of the war in Iraq, that "combat phase" that had never ended. Beside him was L. Paul Bremer, the bold and bumbling proconsul under whose regency the insurgency had taken root and flourished. And beside Bremer, finally, stood George Tenet, the director of central intelligence whose long tenure will be known to history as twice distinguished—by the failure to detect the coming 9/11 attacks and by the certainty about Iraq's bristling arsenal of weapons of mass destruction, those magical objects that, having provided the *casus belli* for the war, turned out not to exist. The three men, dedicated public servants all, had been coauthors of failures quite monumental in their implications, a truth that by December 2004 was quite incontestable, whatever your politics. Now they were receiving from the leader's hands the country's highest civilian honor and basking in the light and warmth of his smile.

That the truth of their failures was incontestable did not matter. The ceremony served not to proclaim truth but rather to assert and embody a proposition that has been central to the current administration: Truth is subservient to power. Power, rightly applied, *makes* truth. As I watched the television screen and murmured that simple formula, the fragment of Orwell that had been dancing just beyond the grasp of my consciousness finally took shape: "History is something to be created rather than learned." In a few moments, even as the freshly bemedaled heroes on the screen were still smiling and shaking hands, I found the full quotation:

From the totalitarian point of view history is something to be created rather than learned. A totalitarian state is in effect a theocracy,
and its ruling caste, in order to keep its position, has to be thought
of as infallible. But since, in practice, no one is infallible, it is frequently necessary to rearrange past events in order to show that
this or that mistake was not made, or that this or that imaginary
triumph actually happened.[1]

These words, written in 1946, are imbued with the anti-
totalitarian struggle, the one just ended and the one about to begin. Six decades later, the United States is far from a totalitarian
state. But we have seen, during these past half dozen years of
perpetual war, more than a little of "the totalitarian point of
view" and more than a few attempts to "rearrange past events in
order to show that this or that mistake was not made, or that
this or that imaginary triumph actually happened." The words
might serve as a succinct and elegant description of much of our
politics—or, better yet, they might be taken as a caption, ready-
made, and placed beneath a photograph of Messrs. Frank, Bremer, and Tenet receiving their medals from a grateful sovereign.

3.

Nearly five years into the Iraq war, at the beginning of a presidential campaign that may well turn on the question of how to
end it, one might be pardoned for forgetting that that war already ended once before. More than four years have passed since
that richly choreographed victory scene on the USS *Abraham
Lincoln* off the coast of San Diego, when the president, clad

jauntily in a flight suit, swaggered across the flight deck, and beneath a banner famously marked "Mission Accomplished," declared: "Major combat operations in Iraq have ended. In the battle of Iraq, the United States and our allies have prevailed."

At first glance, the grand spectacle of May 1, 2003, fits handily into the history of the pageantries of power. Indeed, with its waving banners and thousands of cheering, uniformed extras gathered on the flight deck of that mammoth aircraft carrier, which had to be precisely turned so that the skyline of San Diego, a few miles off, would not be glimpsed by the television audience—this grand event, in its vast conception and its clockwork staging, in its melding of event and image-of-the-event, would have been quite familiar to the great propagandists of the last century (most notably Leni Riefenstahl, who achieved a similar grandeur of image in her 1934 masterpiece, *Triumph of the Will*). Indeed, however vast and impressive, the May 1 extravaganza seems a propaganda event of a traditional sort, meant to bind the country together in a second precise image of victory (after the carefully staged dethroning of Saddam's statue in Baghdad two weeks before)—a triumphant image intended to fit neatly into campaign ads for the 2004 election. The president was the star, the sailors and airmen and their enormous dreadnought props in his extravaganza.

For all the historic resonances, though, one can't help detecting something different here, a kind of . . . *knowingness*, perhaps even an ironic self-awareness, that would have been unthinkable in 1934. For we have today leaders who are not only radical in their attitudes toward power and truth, rhetoric and reality, but are occasionally willing, to our great benefit, to state this attitude clearly—at least to members of an elite who are thought to have the wit to understand it and to lack the power to do anything about it. In the annals of such frank expressions of the philosophy of power, pride of place must surely be given to this, my favorite quotation of the present age, published in the *New York Times Magazine* on October 17, 2004, by the writer Ron Suskind, who recounts his discussion with the proverbial "unnamed Administration official," as follows:

> The aide said that guys like me were "in what we call the reality-based community," which he defined as people who "believe that solutions emerge from your judicious study of discernible reality." I nodded and murmured something about enlightenment principles and empiricism. He cut me off. "That's not the way the world really works anymore," he continued. "We're an empire now, and when we act, we create our own reality. And while you're studying that reality—judiciously, as you will—we'll act again, creating other new realities, which you can study too, and that's how things will sort out. We're history's actors . . . and you, all of you, will be left to just study what we do."

These words from "Bush's Brain"—for the unnamed official speaking to Suskind is widely known to have been none other than the selfsame architect of the aircraft-carrier moment, Karl Rove—sketch out with breathtaking frankness a radical view in which power frankly determines reality, and rhetoric, the science of flounces and folderols, follows meekly and subserviently in its train. Those in the "reality-based community"—those such as we—are figures a mite pathetic, for all of our adherence to Enlightenment principles and our scurrying after empirical proof proves only that we have failed to realize the singular new principle of the new age: Power has made reality its bitch.

Given such sweeping claims for power, it is hard to expect much respect for truth (or perhaps it should be "truth," in knowing, self-mocking quotation marks); for when you can alter reality at will, why pay much attention to the matter of fidelity in describing it? What faith, after all, is owed to the bitch that is wholly in your power, a creature of your own creation?

That relativist conviction—that what the unenlightened naïvely call "objective truth" is in fact "a discourse" subservient to power, shaped and ordered by the ruling institutions of our society is by no means new; on the contrary, it has served for decades as the fertile truism at the root of much fashionable academic discourse. Leading humanist theorists of the last three decades, European and American both, might concede an intellectual kinship, not least in the disdain for the unimaginative drones of the "reality-based community"—though perhaps they would find themselves a bit nonplussed to discover the idea so blithely put forward by a finely tailored man sitting in a White House office. Accusing power is one thing, quite another when power feels comfortable enough to confess.

4.

We are so embedded in its age that it is easy to forget the stark, overwhelming shock of it: Nineteen young men with box cutters seized enormous transcontinental airliners and *brought those towers down*. In an age in which we have become accustomed to two, three, four, five suicide attacks in a single day—in which these multiple attacks in Iraq often don't even make the front pages of our newspapers—one must make an effort to summon back the openmouthed, stark staring disbelief at that impossible image: the second airliner disappearing into the great office tower, almost weirdly absorbed by it, and emerging, transformed into a great yellow-and-red blossom of flame, on the other side; and then, half an hour later, the astonishing flowering collapse of the hundred-story structure, metamorphosing, in a dozen seconds, from mighty tower to great plume of heaven-reaching white smoke.

The image remains, will always remain, with us; for truly the weapon that day was not box cutters in the hands of nineteen young men, nor airliners at their command. The weapon that day was the television set. It was the television set that made the image possible, and inextinguishable. If terror is first of all a way of talking—the propaganda of the deed, indeed—then that day the television was the indispensable conveyer of the conversation: the recruitment poster for fundamentalism, the only symbolic arena in which America's weakness and vulnerability could be dramatized on an adequate scale. Terror—as Menachem Begin, the late Israeli prime minister and former anti-British terrorist, remarked in his memoirs—terror is about "destroying the prestige" of the imperial regime; terror is about dirtying the face of power.

President Bush and his lieutenants surely realized this, and it is in that knowledge, I believe, that we must find the beginning of the answer to one of the more intriguing puzzles of these last few years: What exactly lay at the root of the almost fanatical determination of administration officials to attack and occupy Iraq? It was, obviously, the classic "overdetermined" decision, a tangle of fear, in the form of those infamous weapons of mass destruction; of imperial ambition, in the form of the neoconservative project to "remake the Middle East"; and of realpolitik, in the form of the "vital interest" of securing the industrial world's oil supplies.

In the beginning, though, was the felt need on the part of our nation's leaders, men and women so worshipful of the idea of power and its ability to remake reality itself, to restore the nation's prestige, to wipe clean that dirtied face. Henry Kissinger, a confidant of the president, when asked by Bush's speechwriter why he had supported the Iraq war, responded: "Because Afghanistan was not enough." The radical Islamists, he said, want to humiliate us. "And we need to humiliate them." For the sake of American prestige and thus of American power, the presiding image of the War on Terror—the burning, smoking towers collapsing into rubble—had to be supplanted by another, of American tanks rumbling proudly down the streets of a vanquished Arab capital. It is no accident that Secretary of Defense Donald Rumsfeld, at the first "war cabinet" meeting at Camp David the Saturday after the 9/11 attacks, fretted over the "lack of targets" in Afghanistan and wondered whether we "shouldn't do Iraq first." He wanted to see those advancing tanks marching across the world's television screens, and soon.

In the end, of course, the enemy preferred not to fight with tanks, though they were perfectly happy to have the Americans do so, the better to destroy these multi-million-dollar anachronisms with improvised explosive devices, so-called IEDs, costing a few hundred dollars apiece. Such is the practice of asymmetrical warfare, by which the very weak contrive to use the strengths of the very strong against them. In the post–Cold War world, after all, as one neoconservative theorist explained shortly after 9/11, the United States was enjoying a rare "unipolar moment." It deployed the greatest military and economic power the world had ever seen. It spent more on its weapons, its army, navy, and air force, than the rest of the world combined. Indeed, the confident assumption of this so-called preponderance was what lay behind the philosophy of power enunciated by Bush's Brain, and what produced an attitude toward international law and alliances that is quite unprecedented in American history. "Our strength as a nation-state," reads the National Security Strategy of the United States of 2005, "will continue to be challenged by those who employ a strategy of the weak using international fora, judicial processes and terrorism." A remarkable troika, these "weapons of the weak," comprising as it does the United Nations and like institutions ("international fora"), international and domestic courts ("judicial processes"), and . . . terrorism. This strange grouping, put forward as the official policy of the United States, is borne of the idea that power is, in fact, everything: the only thing. In such a world, international institutions and courts—indeed, law itself—can only limit the power of the most powerful state. Wielding preponderant power, what need has such a state for law? The latter must be, by definition, a weapon of the weak. The most powerful state, after all, makes reality.

5.

Now consider for a moment this astonishing fact: Little more than a decade-and-a-half into this "uni-polar moment," the greatest military power in the history of the world stands on the brink of defeat. In Iraq, its vastly expensive and all-powerful military has been humbled by a congeries of secret organizations fighting mainly by means of suicide vests, car bombs, and improvised explosive devices—all of them cheap, simple, and effective, indeed so effective that these techniques now comprise a kind of ready-made insurgency kit freely available on the

Internet and spreading in popularity around the world, most obviously to Afghanistan, that land of few targets.

Nearly five years into the Iraq war, the leaders of one of our two major political parties advocate the withdrawal of American combat forces from Iraq, and many in the other party are yielding to the growing urge to go along. As for the Bush administration's broader War on Terror, as the State Department detailed recently in its annual report on terrorism, the number of attacks worldwide has never been higher, nor the attacks themselves more deadly. True, the terrorists of al Qaeda have not attacked again within the United States. Perhaps they do not need to. They are alive and, though decentralized and dispersed—transformed into what might be called "virtual al Qaeda"—in numbers they seem to be flourishing. Their goal, after all, notwithstanding the rhetoric of the Bush administration, was not simply to kill as many Americans as possible but, by challenging the United States in spectacular fashion, to recruit greater numbers to their cause and to move their insurgency into the heart of the Middle East. And these things they have managed to do.

Not without help, of course: In their choice of enemy, one might say that the terrorists of al Qaeda had a great deal of dumb luck, for they attacked a country that happened to be run by leaders who had a radical conception of the potency of power. At the heart of the principle of asymmetric warfare—al Qaeda's kind of warfare—is the notion of using your enemy's power against him. How does a small group of insurgents without an army, without heavy weapons, defeat the greatest conventional military force the world has ever known? How do you defeat such an army if you don't have an army? The answer is obvious: You borrow your enemy's. And this is precisely what al Qaeda did. Using the classic strategy of provocation, the group tried to tempt the superpower into its adopted home-land. The original strategy behind the 9/11 attacks—apart from humbling the superpower and creating the greatest recruiting poster the world had ever seen—was to lure the United States into a ground war in Afghanistan, where the one remaining su-perpower was to be trapped, stranded, and destroyed, as the So-viet Union had been a decade before. (It was to prepare for this war that Osama bin Laden arranged for the assassination, two days before 9/11—via bombs secreted in the video cameras of two terrorists posing as reporters—of the Afghan Northern Al-liance leader and U.S. ally Ahmed Shah Massood.)

Well aware of the Soviets' Afghanistan debacle—the CIA had after all supplied most of the weapons that defeated the Soviets there—Bush administration officials confined the American role to sending plenty of air support, lots of cash, and very few troops, relying instead on its Afghan allies, a strategy that avoided a planned quagmire at the cost of letting al Qaeda's leaders escape. Bin Laden would soon be granted a far more valuable gift: the invasion of Iraq, a country that, unlike Afghanistan, lies at the heart of the Middle East and sits squarely on the critical Sunni-Shia divide—perfectly positioned to fulfill al Qaeda's dream of igniting a regional civil war. It is upon that precipice that we find ourselves teetering today.

6.

Critical to this strange and unlikely history were the administra-tion's peculiar ideas about power: "We're an Empire now and when we act we create our own reality." Power, untrammeled by law or custom; power, unlimited by the so-called weapons of the weak, be they international institutions, courts, or terrorism—power can remake reality. It is no accident that one of Karl Rove's heroes is President William McKinley, who stood at the apex of America's first imperial moment and led the country into a glorious colonial adventure in the Philippines that was also meant to be the military equivalent of a stroll in the park and that led, in the event, to several years of bloody insurgency—an insurgency, it bears noticing, that was fought with extensive use of torture, notably water-boarding, which has made its reappearance in the imperial battles of our own times.

If we are an empire now, as Mr. Rove insists, perhaps it is worth adding that we remain a democracy. And therein lies the rub. A democratic empire, as the Athenians were first to discover, is an odd beast, like one of those mythological creatures born of man and horse. Its power, however great, depends finally on public support. If its leader longs to invade Iraq to restore the empire's prestige and power, he must first convince his people. And at his peril; for if the menacing weapons vanish, if promised cakewalk turns to long and grinding war, the leader's power wanes and support for his war collapses. The empire's greatest vulnerability—a matter not of arms but of politics—is revealed, to be exploited by a clever enemy. Bin Laden in his writings has long focused on Americans' "lack of will," though one doubts even he could have imagined these self-inflicted wounds.

Herein lies a bit of pathos, or a cruel irony: Officials of the Bush administration, now judged by a good part of the public to have lied the country into war, did believe Iraq had weapons of mass destruction, though they shamelessly exaggerated the evidence they had to prove it and the threat those weapons would have posed. Secure in their belief that the underlying threat was real, they felt they needed only to dramatize it a bit to make it clear and convincing to the public—like cops who, certain they have the killer, plant a bit of evidence to "frame a guilty man." If only a few weapons were found, who would care, once the tanks were rumbling triumphantly through Baghdad? By then, the United States military would have created a new reality.

I have a daydream about this. I see a solitary army private—a quartermaster, say, or perhaps a cook—breaking the padlock on some forgotten warehouse on an Iraqi military base and finding a few hundred or a few thousand old chemical artillery shells. They might date from the time of the Gulf War; they might be corroded, leaky, completely unusable. But still they would be "weapons of mass destruction"—to use the misleading and absurd construction that has headlined our age—and my solitary cook or quartermaster would find himself a hero, for he would, all unwittingly, have "proved" the case.

My daydream could easily have come to pass. Why not? It is nigh unto miraculous that the Iraqi regime, even with the help of the United Nations, managed so thoroughly to destroy its once existing stockpile. And if my private had found those leaky shells, and administration officials from the president on down could point to them in triumph, what would have been changed thereby? In fact, the underlying reality would have remained: that, in the months leading up to the war, the administration relentlessly exaggerated the threat Saddam posed to the United States and relentlessly understated the risk the United States would run in invading and occupying Iraq. And it would have remained true and incontestable that—as the quaintly fact-bound British foreign secretary put it eight months before the war, in a secret British cabinet meeting made famous by the so-called Downing Street Memo—"the case [for attacking Iraq] was thin. Saddam was not threatening his neighbors and his WMD capability was less than that of Libya, North Korea or Iran."

Which is to say, the weapons were a rhetorical prop and, satisfying as it has been to see the administration beaten about the head with it, we forget this underlying fact at our peril. The administration needed, wanted, had to have the Iraq war. The weapons were but a symbol, the necessary *casus belli*. Or, to shift from law to cinema, they were what Alfred Hitchcock called the Maguffin (and what Quentin Tarantino, in *Pulp Fiction*, in turn parodied as that glowing mysterious object in the suitcase): that is, a satisfyingly concrete object on which to fasten a rhetorical or narrative end—the narrative end being in this case a war to restore American prestige, project its power, remake the Middle East. Had a handful of those weapons been found, the underlying truth would have remained: Saddam posed nowhere remotely near the threat to the United States that would have justified running the enormous metaphysical risk that a war of choice with Iraq posed. Of course, when you are focused on magical phrases like "preponderant power" and "the uni-polar moment," matters like the numbers of troops at your disposal, and the simple fact that the post–Cold War United States had too few to sustain a long-term occupation of a restive and divided country the size of Iraq, must seem mundane indeed. These facts were the reality, and reality had its revenge; and yet Americans live now in a world in which the magical, glowing image of the weapons has been supplanted not by the truth—the foolishness and recklessness of launching an unnecessary war—but by yet another glowing illusion, of mendacious, dastardly officials who knew the weapons weren't there but touted them anyway.

7.

One of the most painful principles of our age is that scandals are doomed to be revealed—and to remain stinking there before us, unexcised, untreated, unhealed. If this Age of Virtual War has a tragic symbol, then surely this is it: the frozen scandal, doomed to be revealed, and revealed, and revealed, in a never-ending torment familiar to the rock-bound Prometheus and his poor half-eaten liver. All around us we hear the sound of ice breaking, as the accumulated frozen scandals of this administration slowly crack open to reveal their queasy secrets—or rather to reveal that most of them, alas, are not secrets at all.

More than three years have passed since the photographs from Abu Ghraib were first broadcast by CBS News on *Sixty Minutes II* and published by Seymour Hersh in the *New Yorker;* nearly as far back I published a book entitled *Torture and Truth* in which I gathered together Bush administration documents that detailed the decision to use on prisoners in the War on Terror and in Iraq "extreme interrogation techniques"—or, as administration officials prefer to call them, an "alternative set of procedures." A remarkable phrase, this, memorable for its perfect bureaucratic blankness: President Bush personally introduced it to the nation on September 6, 2006, in a full-dress White House speech kicking off the midterm election campaign, at a time when accusing the Democrats of evidencing a continued softness on terror—and a lamentable unwillingness to show the needed harshness in "interrogating terrorists"—appeared to be the Republicans' only possible winning electoral strategy. Indeed, Democrats seemed fully to agree with the president, for they warily chose not to stand in the way of his Military Commissions Act, which appeared to legalize many of these "alternative procedures." And since Democrats did indeed win both houses of Congress, perhaps their victory was owed in part to their refusal to stand in the way of what a less legally and bureaucratically careful politician might call torture. Who can say? What we can say is that if torture today remains a "scandal" or a "crisis," it is so in that same peculiar way that crime or AIDS or global warming or indeed the Iraq war is: that is, they are all things we have learned to live with.

8.

I last visited that war in December, when Baghdad was cold and gray, and I spent a good deal of time drawing black X's through the sources listed in my address book, finding them, one after another, either departed or dead. Baghdad seemed a sad and empty place, with even its customary traffic jams gone, and the periodic, resonating explosions barely attracted glances from those few Iraqis to be found on the streets.

How, in these "words in a time of war," to convey the reality of that place at this time? How to punch through the rhetoric of virtual war—to escape the "political language," as Orwell described it, "designed to make lies sound truthful and murder respectable"? Reading his words, I remember an account from a young Iraqi woman of how that war has touched her and her family. In the blog *Inside Iraq*, this anonymous Baghdadi offers her personal version of what has become a quintessential Iraqi family ritual, making a trip to the morgue. She writes of what lies behind the headlines and the news reports, and her account is what it is.

> We were asked to send the next of kin to whom the remains of my nephew, killed on Monday in a horrific explosion downtown, can be handed over. . . .
>
> So we went, his mum, his other aunt and I. . . .
>
> When we got there, we were given his remains. And remains they were. From the waist down was all they could give us. "We identified him by the cell phone in his pants' pocket. If you want the rest, you will just have to look for yourselves. We don't know what he looks like." . . .
>
> We were led away, and before long a foul stench clogged my nose and I retched. With no more warning we came to a clearing that was probably an inside garden at one time; all round it were patios and rooms with large-pane windows to catch the evening breeze Baghdad is renowned for. But now it had become a slaughterhouse, only instead of cattle, all around were human bodies. On this side; complete bodies; on that side halves; and everywhere body parts.
>
> We were asked what we were looking for; "upper half" replied my companion, for I was rendered speechless. "Over there." We looked for our boy's broken body between tens of other boys' remains; with our bare hands sifting them and turning them.
>
> Millennia later we found him, took both parts home, and began the mourning ceremony.

These are the words of people who find themselves as far as they can possibly be from the idea that, when they act, they "create their own reality"—that they are "history's actors." The voices come from history's objects and it is worthwhile pondering who the subjects are, who exactly is acting upon them.

The car bomb that so changed their lives was not set by Americans; indeed, Americans even now are dying to prevent such things. I remember one of them, a lieutenant, a beautiful young man with a puffy, sleepy face, and the way he looked at me when I asked whether or not he was scared when he went out on patrol—this was in Anbar Province in October 2003, as the insurgency was growing daily more ferocious. I remember him smiling a moment and then saying with evident pity for a reporter's lack of understanding. "This is war. We shoot, they shoot. We shoot, they shoot. Some days they shoot better than we do." He was patient in his answer, smiling sleepily in his young beauty, and I could tell he regarded me as a creature from another world, one who could never understand the world in which he lived. Three days after our interview, an explosion near Fallujah killed him.

Ours is a grim age, still infused with the remnant perfume of imperial dreams. It is a scent Orwell knew well. Contingency, accidents, the metaphysical ironies that seem to stitch history together like a lopsided quilt—all these have no place in the imperial vision. A perception of one's self as "history's actor" leaves no place for them. But they exist, and it is invariably others, closer to the ground, who see them, know them, and suffer their consequences.

An Egregious
Collocation of Vocables

Patricia J. Williams

At the heart of Orwell's classic essay, "Politics and the English Language," is his fear that the unconsidered use of language makes it easier to "have foolish thoughts." Foolish thoughts, in turn, make one susceptible to political manipulation whose end is "to make lies sound truthful and murder respectable, and to give an appearance of solidity to pure wind."

When I first read this essay in high school, Stalinism, Fascism, and McCarthyism were more or less things of the past, and the Soviet Union was Someplace Else Entirely. I viewed his warning about empty words as the punishingly academic exercise of a bad-tempered martinet. Orwell did not speak to my unswerving determination to rescue terms like "grooving" from underutilization.

Now, of course, I know that Orwell (unlike my English teacher) wasn't denouncing sloppy language simply for the sake of grammatical symmetry. He worried about a loss of interpretive skills when the mind is submersed in a soothing mash of clichés, soft and well-worn as cushions. What was at stake for him was the discipline of communicative syntax. He valued precision not for its own sake but rather because he thought careless slippage confounded the algebraic equations of deeper meaning.

Vexed as he was by Latinate enfrillments and vrai-Saxon bons mots, many of Orwell's examples sound a bit precious by today's metric of woe. For all that, George Orwell would have had no trouble cutting through the cowpokey folksiness and spewed malapropisms of President George W. Bush. In 1946, it was the "effete languors of Langham Place" (meaning the Etonian swells at the BBC) that lulled one into apolitical slumber. Orwell, I think, would have seen that in today's America it is the argot of the straight-shooting, plain-speaking Average Joe that is exploited for its divine political somnambulism. "Pretentious diction" was not offensive to him because it sounded ridiculously highfalutin, but because it lent "an air of scientific impartiality to biased judgments." His emphasis, in other words, was as much on the pretense in pretension as on the dictum in the diction.

After all, the real Eric Arthur Blair, writing under the pen name George Orwell, was himself a professional propagandist who earned his chops producing purportedly impartial BBC broadcasts that were in fact engineered efforts to provoke colonial India into war against Japan. The experience left him with an intense dislike of such manipulation. He feared polemics that were purposely devoid of signification even as their multisyllabic surface glittered with promise of complexity.

Orwell also knew that potent new devices of propaganda were emerging—new means of public hypnosis and mass influence, to say nothing of media-dispensed distraction. Machiavelli notwithstanding, this scientifically enhanced power to dictate political division and create desire was still very recent when Orwell wrote. The sociological insight derived from widespread data gathering and demographic analysis wasn't even a coherent body of study until the 1930s; hence, Orwell's vision was just short of prophetic. As the hero in Orwell's 1939 novel *Coming Up for Air* said about Hitler and Stalin: "They aren't like these chaps in the old days who crucified people and chopped their heads off and so forth, just for the fun of it— They're something quite new—something that's never been heard of before."

Today, the Bush administration's mangled, tangled declarations of a sprawling War on Terror have marked a watershed in the corruption of political language. The laws, policies, and executive orders that have flowed from this administration are testament to the dizzying array of "mental vices" that Orwell so abhorred. Suddenly we live in a world of bright-lined Good Guys and Bad Guys. Our "quickie" "cakewalk" of a foray into Iraq has morphed into a "decades-long" adventure that has left an untold civilian death count, ruined museums, shattered mosques, plundered archeological sites, and devastated universities throughout Iraq, and whose ongoing brutality risks flattening every home, every block, every city in that nation. "Back to the Stone Age," as Richard Armitage is said to have threatened President Musharraf if Pakistan failed to cooperate with American interests. America the Beautiful, meanwhile, has become a "homeland" secured; and our constitutive text is less the U.S. Constitution than a shadow document called the USA PATRIOT Act. No longer is the collective discourse one of competing theories of constitutional interpretation. These days it is a rivalry between completely different textual universes: between due process and none at all; between the courts and unfettered executive discretion; between personal privacy and super-surveillance; between public accountability and official holes of dark and unfathomable secrecy.

Orwell was always making lists of rules or pseudo-rules that embodied imperiled values as he saw it—the five rules for a politics of language, the seven shrinking commandments in Animal House ("All animals are equal, but some animals are more equal than others"), the enumerated slogans of Newspeak in *1984,* ("WAR IS PEACE; FREEDOM IS SLAVERY; IGNORANCE IS STRENGTH"). If I were Orwell observing today's media and political climate, here's what I imagine he might have come up with:

1. *The death of metaphor.* Orwell was worried about "dying metaphors"—analogies so overused that they lose evocative power and signal only laziness on the speaker's part. I worry that today's American vernacular has killed metaphor outright. Mass media have surely enabled this corruption. Television values "plain meanings" over the complex, "bright lines" over shades of gray, and "lowest common denominator" over any calculation. Similarly, fundamentalist religious leaders have divided the world into easy halves of Good and Evil. More and more school systems place the amassing of information above the acquisition of skills in critical analysis.

   Where there is no sense of metaphor at all—no play, no elasticity between a word and its poetic echoes—totalism becomes easier. When this sort of fundamentalism rules in religion, it becomes easier to cast God *as* the word. Blasphemy becomes a palpable harm, and punishable, the grounds for excommunication or holy war. If the Bible says God created the earth in six days, then that's that. An "eye for an eye" becomes justification for killing abortion doctors. Parable turns into mandate, mandate into jihad. Similarly, when linguistic fundamentalism rules in politics, then police power becomes an inflexible taskmaster. "Zero-tolerance" policies depend on a lack of metaphor or interpretive give. How else did we get to the point where any "sharp-pointed object"—from a nail clipper to an Afro pick—can be defined as a "weapon"? The war on substance abuse bars "drugs" from schools? Then you get suspended for having an aspirin in your backpack. The word is infallible, inerrant, literally dictatorial.

If strict textualism tends to rule contemporary American language at the popular level, this general lack of poetic sensibility is ripe for manipulation by the expert rhetoricians who run Madison Avenue and who also write presidential speeches. Phrases like "axis of evil" have been deployed to depict everything from the ACLU to Saddam Hussein to French fries as the work of Satan himself. Who needs diplomacy when Armageddon is at hand? The very term "War on Terror" defies political critique—it appeals to the unconscious rather than to history; its force is located in the sphere of emotions rather than the cycle of history, it is epic and endless rather than discretely circumstantial. Who can vote for health care or education while cowering under the bed?

2. *The wishful immediate.* The loss of the subjunctive in American speech is a much underrated if not altogether invisible cause for worry. With its abandon by the collective culture, any shred of the contingent or conditional has

disappeared as well. No word stands for anything but its plain meaning, and plain meaning runs no further than the present tense. This is a slippage that advertisers have perfected; it is the essence of commercial sloganeering. In this brave new world, all things are possible, all things are present, all fantasies made real. You didn't just wish it were so, it *was*. The present imaginary rewrites the past. This is, I think, symptomatic of a national mood that routinely considers itself only a purchase away from perfection. The American work ethic that for so long promised "anything" as possible has morphed into a wish ethic that tolerates no earthly limit. It is a greedy state of mind, to say the least, but also one that glorifies lying, cheating, and dissembling as a kind of blind ambition. When exploited as a feature of political discourse, it serves to divide us from history, from facts, from sinkholes in the road of life; and floats us gently into Wonderland. "Mission Accomplished!" "Colorblind Society!" If only it were so.

3. *The passive explosive.* Here, the passive voice is used to bury agency and to reassign responsibility; conversely, the active voice is sometimes used to animate the passive. For example, in the weeks before we invaded Iraq, there was endless official iteration of the phrase "It's Saddam's choice." Lord knows, went the subtext, we didn't want to have to go in there and tear the place up, but if Saddam compelled us, well, Saddam was in the driver's seat. It was Saddam who failed to disprove the subsequently disproved rumors of yellow-cake uranium and aluminum rods. No matter that teams of international inspectors had found no

evidence of weapons of mass destruction—Saddam made us do it.

This puppetry of ventriloquized "choice" has cost the Bush administration and the American people. It has even cost us the allegiance of our very best friend in the Muslim world, Afghan president Hamid Kharzai, who recently denounced American maneuvers that resulted in at least ninety civilian deaths within ten days. The American response to this misfortune blamed al Qaeda for "choosing" to blend into civilian populations. It was, therefore, entirely al Qaeda's fault. Anyone else whose lives went up in a puff of smoke was mere unintended "collateral damage."

This is a species of puppetry that short-circuits painful but crucial opportunities to reflect upon the complexities of power and its absolutes. We have dulled our responses to the sharp moral questions we might otherwise have to confront. Consider another example closer to home: Say a glassy-eyed drug addict runs naked through his neighborhood, waving a steak knife and a pair of glow-in-the-dark knitting needles. Police officers arrive and promptly shoot the man dead. Depending on the circumstances, it might be a reasonable reaction or an overreaction, an accident or negligence. But can there be any doubt that one needs to consider more facts, or that there ought to be some detailed scrutiny for ultimate accountability? In the last few years, however, such encounters have increasingly been labeled "police-assisted suicide" or "suicide by cop." This unfortunate terminology shifts all the agency away from a public officer who, justifiably or not, actually made the decision to fire a weapon. It redefines the police as passive extensions of the outlandish will of the deceased. By law, police actions are constrained by the reasonable exercise of force; but why bother with all that if dying was by the crazy person's choice, rather than at the officer's hand?

Similarly, when three uncharged detainees committed suicide in the prison at Guantanamo Bay, our top brass called it "asymmetrical warfare." The erasure of the self was styled as a rudely aggressive affirmative act of warfare against others. Suicide became a peculiar form of public relations propaganda—unfair, out of proportion, designed to make the good guys look bad. While it may indeed constitute bad press, this nomination diverts attention from more serious questions of moral accountability, such as the due process owed even the most reprehensible captives (to say nothing of those with no pending charges) under the Geneva Conventions.

4. *Epocha disputanda.* Whereas Orwell worried about the overuse of foreign words to obfuscate what is not implied, I worry about the use of foreign places, mythic times, and distant planets to do the same job. This or that happened long ago, under someone else's watch, not on American soil, or in a free trade zone where all of the usual rules were suspended. The Bush-Cheney administration has been masterful in the use of the epochal tense to obliterate causal connection. The president cut a nobler profile than Buzz Lightyear as he promised a manned mission to Mars—to the future and beyond!—even as he installed a head of NASA who doesn't believe there's any such thing as global warming. Similarly, distant times and places-that-never-were are constructed to isolate indiscretions. Recently, the

CIA was forced to declassify thousands of files that document assassinations, use of unwitting citizens for drug experimentation, illegal wiretapping, sabotage of lawful political groups, and torture. The documents, according to a spokesman, "provide a glimpse of a very different time and a very different agency." Ah, the distant, mythic agency long gone, the limbic otherworld of epic creatures. As in the Aeneid, we are transported to another dimension: I sing of arms and the man and the CIA.

5. *Whatever goes on two legs is an enemy.* Growing up as a good little girl of the Cold War era, I learned to fear the KGB. We read about Stalin and the temperamental Mr. Khrushchev; we welcomed the exiled novelists and dancers and athletes who fled from behind the Iron Curtain. The USSR, we were told, was oppressive because of its system of secret police, its inhuman gulags and lack of due process. It is therefore quite astonishing to wake up and find our Bill of Rights effectively upended by so-called signing papers, unchecked executive privilege, unwarranted data mining, whimsical fishing expeditions, and secret searches of people's homes. Not only are citizens not "secure in their papers," as the Fourth Amendment puts it, but neither are they secure in their computers, cell phones, automobile global positioning chips, elevator monitors, Medi-alert beepers, credit cards, nannycams, tracking devices, or DNA trails. In a land where everyone's a suspect, there's suddenly probable cause to search everyone.

This high-tech voyeurism has any number of unsettling consequences. In an executive branch dominated by fundamentalist Christians whose mission is determined to break down all boundary between church and state, the Doctrine of Total Depravity seems to be displacing the presumption of innocence. It also seems to operate as a kind of theoretical underpinning for the administration's use of preemptive detention as a justifiable check upon humanity's inherent transgressivity. In different but parallel evolution, youth culture revels heedlessly in the cyber-exposure of MySpace, Facebook, and YouTube. Even as intelligence agencies troll the Internet for foolish and illegal behavior, a whole generation positively frolics in the gaze of the panopticon, seemingly bent upon memorializing themselves naked, with bongs. There's an odd Village-y Communism about it—no secrets here! It is as though the in-your-face voyeurism of Spring Break has become a righteous political stance. Perhaps none of this is any different from the antics of Careless Youth throughout the ages—the bearded, bare-breasted hordes at Woodstock certainly frightened my parents. But it's worth wondering if we are not seeing a new brand of creative accommodation to totalistic oversight.

6. *The rupture of the Rapture.* The narrative of the Rapture has been popularized in recent years by Timothy LaHaye's global best-sellers, the Left Behind series. Although fiction is, after all, just fiction, these books are some of the most widely read in the world, and their apocalyptic inclination does seem to reflect something beyond the bounds of a given genre. The narrative of the Rapture predicts that when God finally rains down his long-overdue wrath, the sanctified-in-Christ will rise to Heaven, and the sluggardly

nonbelievers will be "left behind" to perish in eternal flame. LaHaye's books propagandize this doomsday scenario by casting the Devil as the secretary of the United Nations. The United Nations stands in for the Tower of Babel. Peace among the nations of the earth is really only a Satanic plot to make good principled Christians settle for heathenish relativism and the dilution of the tribes.

IN A WORLD as rigidly literal as ours, however, these images don't always resonate as mere tropes, or even as fictive. They are circulated within a Fox-and-fear-driven media brew where widely watched televangelists like Pat Robertson or the late Jerry Falwell can roar that the devastation of Hurricane Katrina was not merely an "act of God" but the premeditated intervention of a punitive God. A God, who, like Zeus with his thunderbolts, took specific aim at the Chocolate City of Sin, where far too many good times and way too much mumbo gumbo had long been allowed to roll. New Orleans, in other words, simply got what it deserved.

Religion aside, however, the political employ of "just deserts" has enjoyed renewed and growing currency since the Reagan years. The loaded, coded reference to those who are "deserving" as opposed to "undeserving" rationalizes the status quo of a citizenry divided between an earthly heavens and hells—that is, between suburban utopia and ghetto squalor, good white families and bad black men, the rights-endowed and "aliens," the innately intelligent and dumb savage brutes, civilized taxpayers and the lazy underclass. The sense of divine inevitability that informs this civic vision allows us to wash our hands of a whole raft of otherwise obvious political and biblical injunctions: feed the poor, heal the sick, educate the illiterate, house the homeless, rehabilitate the wounded. Instead, we have watched the divisions in the United States grow wider and wider. The distance between rich and poor has never been greater. The size of the prison population has never been bigger. Nationally, public schools are more segregated than they were in 1954 when the *Brown* case was decided. And health insurance has never been more expensive.

This tragic ongoing split in American society erupts from time to time—in riots, in immigration crises, in racist gang fights, in outbreaks of disease, in appalling rates of infant mortality, in the manifest negligence that allowed the city of New Orleans to drown.

Orwell feared Communism, Fascism, Totalitarianism, and all their attendant linguistic conceits. What he did not foresee, perhaps, was a privatized but global corporate oligarchy whose police power comes wrapped in a sheepish ideology of laissez-faire, sanctified as God's will.

Freedom, Liberty, and Rights:
Three Cautionary Tales

ARYEH NEIER

In 2002, a year after the terrorist attacks on New York City and Washington, D.C., the Bush administration published a new version of "The National Security Strategy of the United States of America." That document helped to signal the administration's intent to launch a war against Iraq by asserting the readiness of the United States to engage in preemptive wars against its designated enemies even where it did not face an imminent threat.

Preemption was, of course, the focus of public attention on the National Security Strategy. Yet the document is also notable for the frequency with which it uses the words *freedom, liberty,* and *rights* to describe American policies and America's position in the world. The opening sentences of the introduction by President Bush invoke a messianic struggle between light and darkness:

The great struggles of the twentieth century between liberty and Totalitarianism ended with a decisive victory for the forces of freedom—and a single sustainable model for national success: freedom,

49

democracy and free enterprise. In the twenty-first century, only nations that share a commitment to protecting basic human rights and guaranteeing political and economic freedom will be able to unleash the potential of their people and assure their future prosperity.

Though I have devoted my career to trying to protect rights, this was a disquieting statement. I think of rights as limits on power. We delegate certain powers to the state to promote the common good, but those powers do not include—or so says the United States Constitution—the power to stop us from expressing our thoughts; or the power to punish us unfairly; or the power to torture us or invade our privacy; or to deny us the equal protection of the laws. These are our rights. We are free because we can exercise these rights. We enjoy liberty because we can secure protection of these rights when they are threatened.

A "decisive victory for the forces of freedom" is another matter. In this rendering, freedom is not merely a limit on power. Rather, it is an instrument of power. Cast as an ideology—almost fetishized—freedom is said to have triumphed over its enemies because of its superior virtue. This is made clear by the next phrase, which claims that, in the wake of this victory, there is only "a single sustainable model for success: freedom, democracy and free enterprise." Those overcome by the forces of freedom have no choice but to accept the only true faith.

Twenty years earlier, in June 1982, President Ronald Reagan made a speech to the British Parliament in which he launched what he called a "crusade for freedom." Reagan's main focus at the time was on the Cold War struggle with the Soviet Union and the armed conflicts in Central America that he saw as part of that struggle. As the speech did not deal with the Middle East, Reagan's choice of words did not attract much comment at the time. Yet if you set President Bush's introduction to the 2002 National Security Strategy alongside President Reagan's 1982 speech at Westminster, it is apparent that Bush's "decisive victory" and "single sustainable model" are a continuation of Reagan's "crusade." In both cases, "freedom" is a weapon of war to vanquish infidels. President Bush's frequent assertions that terrorists hate America's freedoms and are trying to destroy "our way of life" seems to reflect his view that al Qaeda sees the current struggle the same way.

Another significant aspect of President Bush's introduction to the National Security Strategy is that it brackets "free enterprise" and "economic freedom" with political freedom. Indeed, the National Security Strategy goes on to say, "The concept of 'free trade' arose as a *moral principle* even before it became a pillar of economics" [emphasis added]. For the Bush administration, free trade is not just good economic policy; it is, in common with other moral principles, sacrosanct. Those who do not support free trade are, therefore, guilty of sacrilege. The religious basis of the Bush administration's commitment to freedom was underscored in the president's second inaugural address, delivered on January 20, 2005, in which he said that "every man and woman on this Earth has rights, and dignity and matchless value because they bear the image of the maker of heaven and earth." Freedom would triumph, the president continued, because "history also has a visible direction set by liberty and the author of liberty."

The Bush administration and its allies may be the most obvious abusers of the words *freedom, liberty,* and *rights,* but talk of "rights" is also pervasive on the left. Their use of the term is not restricted to the civil and political rights identified in the French Declaration of Rights of 1789 or the American Bill of

Rights of 1791. Those great charters shaped the views of those who think of rights as limits on the state. The French declaration proclaimed the presumption of innocence, while the first ten amendments to the American Constitution set forth the protections to which all are entitled before they may be subjected to a criminal penalty; and both charters guaranteed that each of us may speak, write, publish, or worship without the interference of the state. The French declaration also asserted that all are equal in rights, whereas in the American case, it was only in a further series of amendments, adopted following the Civil War, that the concept of equal rights was incorporated into the Constitution.

Today, however, it is customary on the left to add a great many rights to those enumerated in the French Declaration of Rights or the American Bill of Rights, supplemented by the Thirteenth, Fourteenth, and Fifteenth Amendments that abolished slavery and recognized equal rights. These additional rights include economic rights, such as a "right to health care," a "right to housing," and a "right to food," and what are sometimes called "third-generation rights" such as the "right to a healthy environment." Yet calling such matters rights raises profound questions about what is meant by rights. The effort by the left to equate economic rights with traditional civil and political rights is the mirror image of the effort by the Bush administration to equate free trade and economic freedom with political freedom. Although economic freedom and economic rights sound similar, they actually signify opposite approaches. The champions of economic freedom contend that there may be no restraints on the uses of capital. On the other side, the proponents of economic rights not only want to restrain the way that capital is used but also to require its redistribution as a matter of rights.

USE OF THE TERM *rights* to deal with economic issues is a worldwide phenomenon. The obvious inability of poor countries to provide all the benefits that the left has designated as rights has not acted as a restraint. Instead, it has given birth to other concepts. One is that rights should be realized progressively as countries acquire the necessary resources for economic development. The other is that there is yet another right: a so-called right to development. Implementation of this right requires the transfer of resources from countries that are wealthy to those that are poor.

As an example of the way economic rights would work, consider the question of the right to health care. One person may require kidney dialysis, another may need a heart bypass operation, another may have to have long-term cancer care, and yet another may need lifelong anti-retroviral therapy. In each case, failure to provide this care would probably mean that the person who needs it will die. Surely, therefore, if health care is a right, the state has an obligation to provide such treatment to each of these persons and all others who have similar needs. Moreover, the manner in which such care is provided should meet a high standard. That heart bypass operation, for example, should be conducted by a well-qualified surgeon operating in facilities where it is possible to cope with any unexpected complications.

As should be evident, substantial resources that lie well beyond the reach of most countries are required to provide such care. In my view, a wealthy country such as the United States should, as a matter of good public policy, provide such care to all citizens who need it. Yet to achieve this even in the United States, unless public spending on health care were greatly increased, deep cuts would have to be made in spending on primary health care. If total spending on health care were increased to the degree required for both life-saving care for the chronically ill as well as primary care for all, there would seem to be two alternative ways to cover the extra costs. One would be to decrease spending on other aspects of government, for example, on education, transportation, criminal justice, or national security; the other would be to increase taxes. As a citizen, I espouse the shifts in spending priorities and in tax policy needed to provide comprehensive health care for all. Where I have difficulty, however, is with the idea that those with different views should have no say in the matter because, as with the Bush administration's position on free trade, a moral principle, or a right, has been invoked. The intended effect of spelling out civil and political rights in the American Bill of Rights and the French Declaration of Rights was to make it clear that there is no justification for their abridgment. Rights trump all other policy considerations. Those on the left who place matters such as housing, health care, or the environment on the same plane and call them rights proclaim that they can be dealt with in the same way. They cannot be subjected to policy determinations. They, too, should be outside the realm of democratic decisionmaking, as is made plain by the first five words of the American Bill of Rights concerning civil and political rights: "Congress shall make no law. . . ."

The concept of progressive realization of rights, which is favored by many on the left as a way to deal with the difficulty of implementing economic rights in poor countries, makes nonsense out of the idea of rights. In the process of recognizing that these so-called rights are dependent on economic resources, it undermines the principle that rights always take precedence over all other considerations. The implication is that such rights as freedom of speech, freedom of the press, and the right not to be subjected to cruel treatment may also be limited when states lack resources or when they come into conflict with other considerations. Indeed, many repressive governments have caught on and justify denials of civil and political rights on the ground that they are developing countries and, therefore, are not able to respect such rights as freedom of expression.

As to a right to development—another of those third-generation rights—this would require the establishment of a global authority capable of enforcing it by requiring and overseeing the transfer of resources from the wealthy parts of the world to the poor. Aside from the fact that there is little or no prospect of the establishment of such an authority, one wonders whether any of those who use the term *rights* in this context have thought about the impact it would have on rights if it were to be established.

Unfortunately, promiscuous use of the term *rights* is enshrined in international law. Articles 22 through 26 of the Universal Declaration of Human Rights, adopted by a resolution of the United Nations in 1948, set forth a number of economic and social rights. And a more comprehensive list of such rights appears in the International Covenant on Economic, Social and Cultural Rights, which has been ratified by most governments worldwide (not by the United States, however), though this has had no significant impact in making available the benefits supposedly guaranteed by this treaty to those lacking them. Other international agreements also recognize such rights, as do a number of national constitutions. Their recognition on a national basis has had only a little more impact in practice than their incorporation in international treaties. Despite the evident difficulty of enforcing such "rights," they enjoy extensive rhetorical support on the left. It has reached the point that even when rights advocates argue that this is a misuse of the term, they are considered heretical by many on the left.

Orwell wrote, "But if thought corrupts language, language can also corrupt thought." The way that words such as *freedom*, *liberty*, and *rights* are now used seems to me to illustrate his point. Our government uses them to proclaim its virtue and its power, and both the government and its opponents on the left in all parts of the world use them to insist that the economic policies they favor are beyond debate. In the process, both sides diminish the value of these words in expressing the need to limit power, question exclusive claims to virtue, and foster debate.

Sloppiness and
the English Language

FRANCINE PROSE

I suppose it's a sad commentary on our cultural moment that I should feel so fortunate to be teaching at a college at which the students—my students—can actually read George Orwell's 1946 essay, "Politics and the English Language." Given the current level and health of our educational system, the fact that they can understand what Orwell is saying seems not only unusual but distressingly worthy of mention.

If we are reflecting on the things that Orwell didn't know and perhaps could not have imagined, the widespread inability to read him would be, I would guess, near the top of the list. Most writers (Orwell among them) would be shocked and appalled to learn that, in only sixty years, a large percentage of the population—including many college students—would be unable to fathom the language of a relatively simple and straightforward essay they'd written. The irony, of course, is that Orwell's essay is about language, and about the dangerous ways in which inattention to usage and vocabulary can blunt and disarm our social and political antennae. An additional irony is that Orwell's protest against jargon of every sort should confound students at institutions—academic institutions—at which so many faculty members no longer bother making (or pointing out) the distinction between academic jargon and comprehensible speech.

When I say "read" and "understand," I'm excluding the sections of Orwell's essay (slow going even for most adults) in which Orwell gives examples of the problems he finds in contemporary writing, evidence of the messy language that he believed to be so intimately allied with sloppy thought. The five passages he cites are not only guilty of "avoidable ugliness," "staleness of imagery," and "lack of precision" but are also boring and opaque to the point of impenetrability. The "dying metaphors" to which he objects (*Ring the changes on, take up the cudgels for,* and so forth) are now so long in their graves, and so unlikely to be resurrected, that a student might be understandably mystified to learn that they were ever in common usage, let alone common enough to have become clichés.

Orwell could not have known that his preference for strong, simple verbs (as opposed to longer verbal phrases) would have been so enthusiastically shared and embraced by so many English teachers that, in student fiction, characters are more likely to stride than to walk. And we may feel that Orwell goes a little far in encouraging us to exclude many basic words from our vocabulary (*basic,* in fact, is among them, as is *inevitable, virtual, exhibit,* and *exploit*) for which it is difficult to come up with satisfactory synonyms. We may quarrel with his suggestion that the use of foreign and Latinate words and phrases (as opposed to good old Anglo-Saxon thumpers) are inevitably (oops, *inevitable* is one!) pretentious. I happen to like the word *clandestine,* just as I would argue that *cul-de-sac* is a perfectly acceptable way of saying *dead end.*

Which brings me back to the question of what (happily for him) Orwell didn't know: that the English language would become not only murky, vague, and false but also so impoverished that we would find ourselves thrilled to see—in a student paper or the tabloid press—the occasional Latinate word or a correctly used example of high diction.

Even if Orwell's essay seems, at certain points, to be dated or excessive, it remains as useful and as relevant—as critically important—today as it must have seemed when it was written. The dangers that Orwell was warning his readers against—the ways in which the language of politics can be muddied and distorted in order to make the average literate citizen incapable of thinking clearly or of understanding what he or she is being told—are no less (and perhaps more) threatening than they were in Orwell's day. At the time the piece was written, Fascism had lately been defeated in Germany, and though Russia was in the grip of a totalitarian regime, it did seem unlikely that the dire imaginings of *1984* were about to come true in Great Britain; the novel was published three years after "Politics and the English Language."

Indeed, "Politics and the English Language" seems (to use exactly the sort of cliché that so offended Orwell) as timely as if it had been written yesterday. As we have learned from the history of regimes, including, among others, those of Joseph Stalin and the Argentinean junta, oppression has its own linguistics, shaped and tailored to fit the need to euphemize, pacify, and deceive. Orwell was dead-on about the ways in which adjectives, nouns, and verbs can be perverted for the uses of politics, and about the insidious rapidity in which information can be alchemized into propaganda.

Though I know such people exist, it is hard to imagine a sentient human being who has lived through the Bush-Cheney years without noticing what has been done to terms such as *freedom, patriotism,* and *liberty*—to take just the most blatant examples of words that have been given freighted and false new meanings. The same is true for the word *democracy,* which Orwell himself singled out for particular scrutiny:

> In the case of a word like *democracy,* not only is there no agreed definition, but the attempt to make one is resisted from all sides. It is almost universally felt that when we call a country democratic we are praising it: consequently the defenders of every kind of régime claim that it is a democracy, and fear that they might have to stop using the word if it were tied down to any one meaning. Words of this kind are often used in a consciously dishonest way. That is, the person who uses them has his own private definition, but allows his hearer to think he means something quite different.

Sound familiar? What was it exactly that we went to Iraq to "spread"?

For all these reasons and more, I feel—as we often do with a work of literature—that Orwell's essay was written for me. I don't mean precisely what people often seem to mean when they talk about literature in this way. I don't feel that it speaks to me in some private, particular way, or that I can identify with it, but rather that it was written for me to use as a classroom text. I generally assign it to my students during the first few weeks of a course I teach—a course about the close reading of literature and the equally close scrutiny of the daily newspaper. It is a course about language, about the best uses and worst abuses of language.

I do think it's good mental exercise (like memorizing Latin verbs) for students to follow the way Orwell's mind moves from point to point. And it's also true that I am using Orwell as a kind of authority or backup; if students don't believe me, perhaps they'll believe the author of *1984* and *Animal Farm*, one or both of which they've read. Orwell's point in something that I will tell them again and again through the semester, but Orwell says it in a few, brief eloquent paragraphs that could be excised from the essay and given to students who have trouble with the whole piece:

> In our time, political speech and writing are largely the defence of the indefensible. Things like the continuance of British rule in India, the Russian purges and deportations, the dropping of the atom bombs on Japan, can indeed be defended, but only by arguments which are too brutal for most people to face, and which do not square with the professed aims of political parties. Thus political language has to consist largely of euphemism, question-begging and sheer cloudy vagueness. Defenceless villages are bombarded from the air, the inhabitants driven out into the countryside . . . this is called *pacification*. . . . People are imprisoned for years without trial . . . this is called *elimination of unreliable elements*. . . .

I like to think that when I teach students to read literature, I am helping to foster a new generation of readers. And when I teach them to pay attention to the language that their political leaders are using, and to the language that is used to report the news in the papers and in the media? I like to think I am educating them to resist the verbal sloppiness, the stupidities, and the easy seductions of propaganda.

Perhaps this is not the place to talk about our literacy rates, our overcrowded classrooms, the paucity of our government spending on education, our mind-destroying embrace of bogus educational reforms, and the dictates of a rigid curriculum and standardized testing. Or perhaps it is always and everywhere the place to talk about such things. Perhaps Laura Bush would argue that we are doing a dandy job of educating our children, but more Americans would argue, I think, that we have a serious educational problem. Orwell was very smart, and painfully knowledgeable, about the horrors that are routinely visited on children in the name of education. One of my favorite Orwell essays, "Such Were the Days," is a dispatch from the hell of being a new kid and a bed wetter amid the casual sadism of a British boarding school. But Orwell would probably not have guessed that other, and equally awful, things would be done to our students, and with so little effect. If you don't believe that kids can think, or should think, it seems unlikely that you will educate them in a way that may help them do it better.

If young people are not trained to think and to pay attention to language—and in particular to the language being used to form their ideas and opinions—it seems obvious that they will be more susceptible to the techniques of advertising (repetition, volume, reductive sloganeering, and so on) than to the more challenging processes of reason, common sense, and logic. Clarity of thought and attention to linguistic nuance are essential tools in subverting propaganda. And surely it's not only a few paranoids who have noticed that systematically under-educating a population is one way to insure future generations of men and women qualified to work at the McDonald's or serve on a corporate board without stepping out of line, or asking too many questions, or asking the wrong questions, or knowing what questions to ask.

Orwell's essay (or in any case, what it says) is a hugely useful tool, profoundly helpful in shaping a very different sort of student—one trained to question everything, to scrutinize information and the way in which it is being framed. You might even say that one aim of education is to produce students who can read and understand "Politics and the English Language" and take to heart statements such as the following:

> This invasion of one's mind by ready-made phrases . . . can only be prevented if one is constantly on guard against them, and every such phrase anaesthetises a portion of one's brain.
>
> . . . Political language—and with variations this is true of all political parties, from Conservatives to Anarchists—is designed to make lies sound truthful and murder respectable, and to give an appearance of solidity to pure wind. One cannot change this all in a moment, but one can at least change one's own habits . . .

Students need to read this, to hear it from us—or from Orwell. And it's certainly possible to get that essential message across. Students may just need extra help. If they can read Chaucer, they can certainly deal with Orwell.

Perhaps I should conclude this essay by noting what I've come to realize only in the course of writing it. I set out to consider how much Orwell didn't know, and I've wound up marveling at how much he knew, and how much he can still teach us.

PART TWO

Symbols and Battlegrounds

What Orwell Didn't Know About the Brain, the Mind, and Language

GEORGE LAKOFF

George Orwell will forever be a hero of mine. When I read *1984* in high school, I became sensitized to the workings of propaganda. After more than forty years as a linguist and cognitive scientist, I remain sensitized.

When I first read "Politics and the English Language" as an undergraduate in the late 1950s, I loved it. Nearly fifty years later I find it an anachronism. Why? I, and those in my profession, have learned a lot about the brain, the mind, and language since then. Orwell's essay belongs to an earlier time, a time that lacked our deepening understanding of how the human brain works.

Orwell suffered from what we might now call the "Editor's Fallacy": Bad habits of "foolish thought" and inaccurate, slovenly, dull, pretentious, ungraceful, and meaningless language—the "decay of language"—lead to political propaganda and its effects. If we just "let the meaning choose the word," he claimed, we would all be saved. This is not only false, it is dangerously naïve.

Orwell fell into traps—false views of language: *Meanings are truth conditions. Words have unitary meanings. If people are told the truth, they will reason to the right conclusions—unless they are stupid or ignorant. And ignorance can be cured by truths conveyed in good prose.*

All of that is false. Yet progressives still fall into those traps. Even you, dear reader, may have fallen into them. And even *I* am trying to cure ignorance via truths conveyed in good prose. I am banking on cognitive dissonance—yours! Dissonance between the real brain and the apparent mind. Intellectuals are confident they know their own minds, though they realize they don't know their own brains. But their brains betray their confidence in their minds. Neuroscience and cognitive science reveal a far more interesting picture than Orwell could have guessed.

Probably 98 percent of your reasoning is *un*conscious—what your brain is doing behind the scenes. Reason is inherently emotional. You can't even choose a goal, much less form a plan and carry it out, without a sense that it will satisfy you, not disgust you. Fear and anxiety will affect your plans and your actions. You act differently, and plan differently, out of hope and joy than out of fear and anxiety.

Thought is physical. Learning requires a physical brain change: Receptors for neurotransmitters change at the synapses, which changes neural circuitry. Since thinking is the activation of such circuitry, somewhat different thinking requires a somewhat different brain. Brains change as you use them—even unconsciously. It's as if your car changed as you drove it, say from a stick shift gradually to an automatic.

Thought is physical in another way. It uses the brain's sensory-motor system. Imagining moving uses the same regions of the brain as moving; imagining seeing uses the same regions of the brain as seeing. Meaning is mental simulation, activating those regions of the brain. Reasoning from A to B is the neural activation of the mental simulation of B, given the mental simulation of A. Mental simulation, like most thought, is mostly unconscious.

Thought is structured, in large measure, in terms of "frames"—brain structures that control mental simulation and hence reasoning.

You think metaphorically, perhaps most of the time. Just by functioning with your body in the world as a child, you learn at least hundreds of simple "conceptual metaphors"—metaphors you think with and live by. For example, Quantity is understood in terms of Verticality (More is Up), and the words follow along: *prices rise and fall, skyrocket and hit bottom.* Why? Because every day of your life, if you pour water into a glass, the level rises. You experience a correlation between quantity and verticality. In your brain, regions for registering verticality and quantity are activated together during such experiences. As a result, activation spreads, and circuits linking Verticality to Quantity are formed. Those circuits constitute the metaphor More is Up in your brain. As a child lives in the world, his or her brain acquires hundreds of such "primary" conceptual metaphors that are just there waiting to be used in everyday thought.

We have high-level moral worldviews—modes of reasoning about what's right and wrong—that govern whole areas of reason, both conscious and unconscious, and link up whole networks of frames and metaphors.

Cultural narratives are special cases of such frames. They stretch over time and define protagonists and antagonists—and heroes, victims, and villains. They define right and wrong, and come with emotional content. And most important, we all live out cultural narratives—with all their emotionality and moral sensibility. We even define our identities by the narratives we live by.

What are words? Words are neural links between spoken and written expressions and frames, metaphors, and narratives. When we hear the words, not only their immediate frames and metaphors are activated, but also all the high-level worldviews and associated narratives—with their emotions—are activated. Words are not just words—they activate a huge range of brain mechanisms. Moreover, words don't just activate neutral meanings; they are often defined relative to conservative framings. And our most important political words—*freedom, equality, fairness, opportunity, security, accountability*—name "contested concepts," concepts with a common shared core that is unspecified, which is then extended to most of its cases based on your values. Thus conservative "freedom" is utterly different than progressive "freedom," as I showed in detail in *Whose Freedom*. Liberals such as Paul Starr, in *Freedom's Power*, unselfconsciously use their own version of freedom, as if there were no other version. Not understanding conservative "freedom" and pointing out its problematic nature greatly weakens one's effect.

A few words in political language can activate large portions of the brain: *War on Terror, tax relief, illegal immigration, entitlements* (turned to conservative use by Ronald Reagan), *death tax, property rights, abortion on demand, cut and run, flip-flop, school choice, intelligent design, spending programs, partial birth abortion, surge, spreading freedom, private accounts, individual responsibility, energy independence.*

When they are repeated every day, extensive areas of the brain are activated over and over, and this leads to brain change. Unerasable brain change. Once learned, the new neural structure cannot just be erased: *War on Terror* be gone! It doesn't work. And every time the words are repeated, all the frames and metaphors and worldview structures are activated again and strengthened—because recurring activation strengthens neural connections. Negation doesn't help. "I'm against the War on Terror" just activates the *War on Terror* metaphor and strengthens what you're against. Accepting the language of issue and arguing the other side just hurts your own cause.

Can you counter such brain change? There are two possibilities. First, you can try to mark the idea—as silly, immoral, stupid, and so on—by having lots of people say so over a long period of time. That's what conservatives did with "liberal," starting back in the 1960s when most people wanted to be liberals. *Tax and spend liberal, liberal elite, liberal media, limousine liberal,* and so on repeated over and over slowly got across the idea to lower- and middle-class Republicans that liberals were elite, financially irresponsible, and oppressing poor conservatives. And it undermined liberals' confidence in themselves.

The second strategy is to provide an alternative honest framing—either by inhibiting what is in the brain or by bypassing it. Done honestly, it is righting history. Done dishonestly, it is "rewriting history." Conservatives have done this with the Vietnam War: We lost because we didn't use enough force—*"We had one hand tied behind our backs."*

Neither is quick or easy.

Today, sophisticated right-wing propaganda is very well-written—the editor in Orwell would love David Brooks's prose. Mind control works via brain change, through the effective use of well-written language to activate not just frames, conceptual metaphors, and emotions, but whole worldviews. When the language is repeated and the words become just "the normal way you express the idea," then even the best people in the media get sucked in. Journalists have to use words people understand, and they have to use the words most people normally use to express the ideas they are writing about. As a result, they often have no idea that they are using conservative language, which activates a conservative view of the world as well as the conservative perspective on the given issue. They are rarely aware that in doing so, they are helping conservatives by strengthening the conservative worldview in the public's mind, and thereby accelerating brain change.

Once a member of the public has undergone brain change, he or she then thinks as a conservative on the issue. Not convinced rationally, just subject to the techniques every marketer uses. Is free will being exercised? The very idea of "free will" has been changed.

Orwell wasn't aware of how brains, minds, and language really work, nor was anyone else in 1947. But we don't have that excuse today. Yet even the very best of our news media are stuck in the same traps. Every now and then a result about the brain will leak out into the *Science Times* or *Discover*, only to be forgotten the next week. But what we know about the brain, the mind, and language barely ever makes it to the front page or opinion pages where politics is discussed. The ghost of Orwell still haunts our very best news and political opinion media.

Orwell's old-fashioned views about reason and language also haunt the Democratic Party. But there are promising developments. Presidential candidate John Edwards has rejected the very term *War on Terror* as an inappropriate metaphor and a means to grab power. In the Democratic debate in New Hampshire in June 2007, the questions Wolf Blitzer of CNN asked were all framed from a conservative viewpoint. Democratic candidate Barack Obama stepped forward and rejected *one* of the conservatively framed questions as "specifically designed to divide us."

In another positive development, progressives have been saying out loud that conservatism itself is the problem. Robert Borosage, in *The American Prospect*, staunchly argues from a progressive worldview, "Conservatives cannot be trusted to guide the government they scorn. Not because they are incompetent or corrupt (although corruption and incompetence abound), but because they get the world wrong."

This is half right. But it ignores the thousands of conservative "successes" from *their* point of view, which Borosage cites as "failures." In hundreds of cases (excepting Iraq—a big exception), conservatives would say that George W. Bush got the world right—because he changed the world as he wanted to.[1]

If Democrats think that those who voted for Bush will consider all those "successes" as failures, they might just find a way to lose the next election. Moral: To counter conservatism, you have to understand, and publicly discuss the problems with, the conservative moral worldview. And to do that, you need to know how largely unconscious worldviews work.

Conservative think tanks, over thirty-five years, started with the conservative worldview and showed how to apply it everywhere on every issue, and even beyond issues in the acts of governance—cutting regulating budgets, reassigning regulators, using the courts to redefine the laws, changing the facts on Web sites, eliminating libraries. New Democratic think tanks haven't helped much. The problem is that they are *policy* think tanks. They mistakenly think that "rational" programs and policies constitute political ideas. They don't understand unconscious thought. It's the unspoken ideas behind the programs and the policies—the worldviews, deep frames, metaphors, and cultural narratives—that need to be changed in the public mind. Only one progressive think tank, the Rockridge Institute, is even working in this direction. Its handbook for progressives, *Thinking Points,* applies the study of mind to the cause of truth.

Is it legitimate to use the real mechanisms of mind—worldviews, frames, metaphors, emotions, images, personal stories, and cultural narratives—to tell important truths? Hell, yes! It is usually the only way that works. Al Gore's movie, *An Inconvenient Truth,* uses all those mechanisms of mind and heart—and it works. Had it just given facts and figures unframed, it would have flopped.

It is time to exorcise Orwell's ghost. We all need to understand how the brain, mind, and language really work. We need to apply that knowledge effectively to make truths meaningful and to give *truths* the power to change brains. Our democracy depends on a clear and open understanding of the political mind.

The New Frontier:
The Instruments of Emotion

DREW WESTEN

We usually remember George Orwell for the dangers he foretold about the effective use of propaganda, through which war becomes peace, torture becomes love, ignorance becomes strength, and despots and demagogues elevate euphemism to a high art. That was the George Orwell of *1984*. But Orwell also warned of a very different danger in his classic essay, "Politics and the English Language." Understanding the political climate in the United States in the first several years of the new millennium requires that we understand the Orwell of *1984*, the Orwell who wrote that classic essay on politics and language, and some things about the mind and brain—and the role of television, and hence of sounds and images, and not just words—that Orwell could not have foreseen as a child of the pre-television era.

With the hindsight afforded by history, it's fair to say that Orwell got the title of his book wrong by two decades. His seminal novel should have been called *2004*. The first years of the new millennium were the most Orwellian of American democracy. Polluters drafted a bill which became law, named, as if in a cynical tribute to Orwell, the "Clear Skies Initiative." The president nominated and the Congress acquiesced in the appointment of men who bore the title "Justice" but had no use for it, and who would ultimately resegregate American schools while leaders trumpeted the so-called No Child Left Behind Act. The president and his advisers kept people afraid through precisely the kind of "perpetual war" Orwell described in his novel. George W. Bush sent American soldiers (without adequate body and vehicle armor) to die in the desert of Iraq under false pretenses, guided by political rather than military strategists to determine the size of the occupation force necessary to prevent a foreseeable and foreseen civil war; failed to use diplomacy to secure any solution to a centuries-old conflict; and cut the benefits of veterans who returned home, with damaged lives and limbs, to roach-infested hospitals—all in the name of "supporting our troops."

Of course, in 1984, Nicaraguan death squads came to be called "freedom fighters." But it is unclear to what extent such rhetoric was deliberate deception or simply the ignorance that allows us to be readily blinded by our ideology. As Orwell well understood, confusion of thought and language often go hand and hand, and cause and effect can run in both directions. To be charitable, it seems likely, in 1984, that Ronald Reagan simply could not imagine that someone who called himself a capitalist *and* a friend of the United States could also be a fascist and a bloody dictator. He similarly could not hear the clear message when Daniel Ortega showed in words and deeds that a person could be committed to both democracy (Ortega won a democratic election in a former dictatorship—an election he and his Sandinista government called voluntarily, when they could have gone the way of every other Marxist despot of the twentieth century) and to Marxist ideals far closer to the teachings of Jesus (Ortega was a Jesuit) than Stalin. If you use the words "totalitarian" and "Communist" interchangeably (even though many totalitarian regimes were not, and are not today, Communist), you literally cannot see when the two diverge, particularly when your own nation has been under grave threat for forty years by regimes that are both. I do not profess to know the workings of Reagan's brain, other than that conceptual subtlety, at least in his waning years, was not one of his chief virtues. We know more, however, about "Bush's Brain"[1] and its long history of subterfuge and conscious deception.

Orwell's *1984* described a totalitarian regime, but as he understood, the kind of language we now call "Orwellian" can have effects almost as powerful in a democratic society as in a totalitarian one. In a closed society, one party or despot has control over the instruments of mass communication and the power to enforce its will. Something very similar, however, can happen in a democratic society under specific conditions that are recognizable only in hindsight, although Orwell recognized one of the most important, namely, when a government wages a "perpetual war" that keeps people terrified, focused in their hatred against external and internal enemies, and "patriotic" in the Orwellian sense.

We have seen in the twenty-first century, however, that Orwellian politics can occur in a democracy when one side has economic control of much of the mass media or when journalists are gripped by many of the same emotions as their countrymen, such as fear or hatred, and suspend disbelief. This scenario becomes particularly problematic when the opposition doesn't see what is happening, either, and when it fails to recognize that the media are smuggling Trojan horses into popular discourse from the other side—the circumstance George Lakoff and Kathleen Hall Jamieson emphasize when they talk about frames and media framing. Perhaps the most striking example is the repeated use of the phrase *War on Terror* since the bombing of the World Trade Center on September 11, 2001. The Bush administration carefully crafted this phrase to maximize its fear appeal and to conflate legitimate efforts to combat radical Islamic terrorism with the Iraq war. Not only the media but many Democrats continue to repeat this shibboleth, unaware that it not only activates people's fear of mortality, which inherently shifts people to the right,[2] but also activates associations to the Wizard of Terror (George W. Bush) of 9/11, while deactivating the Straw Man (George W. Bush) of "Mission Accomplished." In so doing, both the media and the Democratic leadership are essentially advertising the "product line" of the Republican Party and selling its "brand." Why Democrats continue to do so after Lakoff warned them about it four years ago is difficult to comprehend, unless you understand how Democrats think about mind and brain (and by extension language, imagery, and metaphor), and how they have failed to grasp the point of Orwell's other masterpiece, "Politics and the English Language."

In that essay, Orwell inveighed against the opposite problem that he emphasized in *1984*, namely, the failure to use language effectively and evocatively. He pointed to empty, hackneyed phrases that might have had an appeal forty years ago but do so no more; the retreat into scientific jargon or Latinate phrases that put readers off and distance them from the feelings the writer intends (or should intend) to evoke; and the use of wordy, turgid prose whose meaning readers must wrest from the writer or speaker like a sword from a stone.

What Orwell could not have foretold is perhaps the primary condition under which Orwellian language can be as effective in a democracy as in a dictatorship: When one side knows how to communicate effectively with the public (and particularly when it is willing to cross the line from effective communication to Orwellian euphemism designed to mislead) and the other side has little idea how to communicate, or when the other side is being outfoxed. This has been the case for most of the forty years since conservatives in the mid-1960s started to hone their language in think tanks, while progressives (who cannot refer to themselves as liberals anymore—perhaps the best index of the imbalance of power in the use of language between the two sides of the political aisle) have been stumbling their way from one emotionally barren message to another. From a communicative standpoint, this situation is no different from a one-party state, because one party controls the instruments of emotion, and emotion drives electoral behavior.[3]

Orwell died young, in 1950, at the advent of the television era, a time when the written word (and increasingly the spoken word on radio) was the lingua franca of political communication. (I just broke one of Orwell's rules—using a foreign phrase when an English one would suffice—but he is not here to slap my hand with a ruler, so I will take the liberty.) What he could not have known was the extent to which the processes he described in language reflect psychological principles similar to those that shape public opinion using visual imagery, music, and intonation in the current era. Our brains are nothing but vast interconnected sets of networks. Of particular importance in political communication are networks of association—bundles of thoughts, feelings, images, memories, motives, and emotions—

that are active outside of awareness but shape conscious thought and behavior, including voting behavior.

Understanding these neural networks is essential to understanding all forms of political communication, linguistic and nonlinguistic (i.e., sensory), because they not only create and collectively comprise "public opinion" but they generate the "overtones" that give much of political messaging its timbre and emotional power. To illustrate the point, let's turn to the actual year 1984, and to one of the most successful political commercials in American history, Ronald Reagan's "Morning in America." This was the first advertisement of his 1984 campaign for reelection, and it set a generally positive, upbeat tone that he maintained throughout the campaign, although it did include an "overtone": The first line was not, as many remember it, "It's morning in America." Rather, the first line read, "It's morning *again* in America [italics added]." That simple phrase activated a network of which most viewers would scarcely be aware, contrasting the clear, sunny morning of Reagan's revitalized America with the dark night of Carter-Mondale's malaise-filled eve. Simply including the word "again" reminded viewers of the question that became the central theme of Reagan's campaign against Carter's vice president: "Are you better off than you were four years ago?"

We can hear the networks whirring in the background if we study the ad itself:

ANNOUNCER: [quiet symphonic music, accompanied by a video of boats pulling out of the harbor in the early morning, against a clean city skyline] It's morning again in America. Today, more men and women [video clip of a smiling businessman stepping out of a taxi on a New York street in the morning, followed briefly by the image of a busy street filled with people heading to work] will go to work than ever [video clip of farmer working the land on his tractor] before in our country's history [video clip of newspaper boy throwing papers from his bike in a suburb, as a smiling man in a tie walks along the sidewalk and waves as a car picks him up for work]. With interest rates at about half the record highs of 1980 [video of a station wagon pulling a small trailer in front of a white paneled home on a large lot], nearly 2,000 families today will buy new homes [video of a man and his young son, with a spring in their steps, carrying a rug into their new home, with a white picket fence increasingly perceptible at the bottom of the screen as the camera pans out, revealing other family members walking briskly and skipping behind them], more than at any time in the past four years. This afternoon [video of a grandmotherly woman with a corsage and a big smile of anticipation on her face, watching a scene about which she is obviously proud and excited] 6,500 young men and women will be married [the video continues, revealing that she is at her granddaughter's wedding, followed by a close-up of the smiling face of the bride, dressed in traditional white with a conspicuous wedding veil] and with inflation at less than half of what it was just four years ago [the video continues, showing the couple embraced in their first kiss as man and wife], they can look forward with confidence to the future [the scene moves to the couple exiting the church, as happy onlookers throw rice, followed by a big hug between the bride and her grandmother]. It's morning again in America [photo of an illuminated White House at dusk, gradually panning out to show a more panoramic view] and under the leadership of President Reagan [video clip of a flag waving in the wind] our country is prouder [video of children looking upward reverently] and stronger [video of a man with a blue shirt and an insignia on his left shoulder, indicating that he is a law enforcement official, pulling the ropes to raise an American flag] and better [video clip of an elderly man proudly raising the flag over his white home]. Why would we ever want to return to where we were [the screen is filled with an American flag waving in the wind] less than four short years ago [the screen reads, simply, "PRESIDENT REAGAN," accompanied by a flag attached to a Reagan button by gold tassels]?[4]

This ad was masterfully crafted to activate multiple networks designed to lead viewers to associate Reagan with all that is positive and good in America. The theme of "morning" activated networks representing a fresh start, the idea that America under Reagan's leadership was experiencing a new day. The ad was filled with images of families, picket fences, weddings, closeness across the generations, and waving flags, all associated (some by culture, and others by a mix of culture and evolution, such as our natural concern for our children) with positive feelings. Without Reagan even speaking a word, the ad emphasized that he was *presidential*, a network activated by the glowing image of the White House, the American flag waving as the announcer uttered the phrase "under the leadership of President Reagan," and the simple message that lingered at the end of the commercial: "PRESIDENT REAGAN." The use of brightness, whiteness, and scenes of morning conveys a freshness and hope that are central to the emotional appeal of the ad. Equally important are the waving flags, which figured prominently in virtually all of Reagan's ads, conveying the theme of American strength and pride restored. This theme was particularly powerful emotionally after what many Americans experienced as their country's humiliation at the hands of a third-rate, Third World nation, Iran, which held seventy Americans hostage for nearly a year-and-a-half before releasing them just as Reagan was about to take office.

The way Reagan wrapped himself and his ideology in the flag, in this ad and throughout his presidency, had another effect that can still be felt today: It created *ambivalence* on the left about the most sacred of all symbols of a nation, its flag.[5] Just as during the Bush era most progressives developed a visceral negative response to the yellow ribbon on the back of cars, designed by conservatives to indicate that they "support our troops" (i.e., support the war in Iraq), Reagan's liberal use of the flag as a symbol of his own party and ideology created a second set of associations to the flag other than the more traditional, positive one: an association to an illiberal, right-wing, jingoistic ideology. Those on the left had already associated the flag with militarism in the 1960s, and had used flag burning as a way of conveying their distaste for the Vietnam War. Unfortunately, this ambivalence remains, if in attenuated form, to this day, and allows conservatives to trot out flag-burning amendments to the Constitution every year at election time as a way of entrapping Democrats who understand the Constitution, even though flag burning occurs in the United States now only about twice a year and hardly merits a constitutional amendment. Most Americans, left and right, learned as children to develop positive feelings linking identification, pride, and community to the flag, leading to as much "internal" flag waving among Democrats as Republicans. But with the exception of the weeks after the attack on the Twin Towers on September 11, 2001, when the level of activation of patriotic feeling in general was especially high, the flag has activated conflicting networks and hence, conflicting feelings on the left, as it represents both our shared sense of community as Americans and the militarism of yellow-ribbon Republicans.

As Reagan's "Morning in America" suggests, the success of an appeal depends not only on the use of words—or the imagery that those words evoke, which we now know activates parts of the cerebral cortex that are involved in the perception and memory of visual scenes. It also depends on the multisensory networks of association a political message evokes. The power of "Morning in America" came not just from its words but from the imagery, the intonation in the narrator's voice, the cadence of his speech, the sounds, and the music. Any appeal— whether a slogan, an ad, a response in a debate, a line from a stump speech, a viral video that travels at warp speed around the Internet—activates and deactivates multiple networks of association. Among the networks that Reagan's ad did not emphasize—and in fact deactivated through its images crossing class lines—were those involving class, and the fact that, economically speaking, it may have been morning in America for those who benefited from his tax cuts and trickle-down economic theories, but it was a very cloudy morning for those who were poor or watched economic disparities skyrocket between rich and poor on Reagan's watch.

By describing the networks activated in "Morning in America," I do not mean to suggest that Reagan or his media team were doing anything illegitimate (although the deactivation of class bordered on it). All communication—political and otherwise—involves the activation and deactivation of networks, and all good political communication associates a candidate or party with positive feelings, associates the opposition with negative feelings, or, as in this case, does both. In "Morning in America,"

Reagan's team simply made its case masterfully to the emotions of the American people.

Reagan did resort elsewhere, however, to unethical appeals, as when he spoke of "welfare queens" and "states' rights" in ways designed to activate under the cover of conscious concerns (about welfare culture and federal control of local decisions) unconscious networks associated with race and prejudice. By 1968, with Nixon's infamous "Southern strategy" (using race to wrest the South from the grip of Democrats), Republicans had discovered that they could activate unconscious networks representing voters' racial prejudices, such as the "scary, violent black male" network, through conscious appeals focusing on welfare, affirmative action, violent crime, and the death penalty (as in the case with the Willie Horton ad run by George H. W. Bush against Michael Dukakis). Republicans did the same thing in 2006 with tremendous effectiveness and complete lack of concern for ethics in the Tennessee Senate race against the black congressman Harold Ford, in which future senator Bob Corker ran an orchestrated campaign about who was the "real Tennessean" (both were from Tennessee) as a conscious cover for a stealth appeal to voters' unconscious prejudices (distinguishing "us" from "them"). The centerpiece of that campaign was the infamous "Call Me" ad put out by the Republican National Committee on Corker's behalf, which featured a white woman whose clothes were not apparent cooing, "I met Harold at a Playboy Party" and reprising at the end, "Harold, call me!" with no purpose other than to activate the network representing the sexually voracious black male with a taste for white women.

As of this writing in late July 2007, similar ads are appearing on YouTube that associate Barack Obama with women of ambiguous race, or morph his face into Osama bin Laden (even calling him

Obamba, activating networks about how African he is and trig-
gering associations with Little Black Sambo). When Roger
Ailes, who was involved in the Willie Horton ad before ultimately developing its natural extension, Fox News, "joked" in
2007 about "Obama sightings" in Pakistan, he knew exactly what
he was doing. The same is true of conservative commentators
such as Ann Coulter, who repeatedly refer to Obama as B. Hussein Obama, creating a double association with dangerous Middle Eastern men. Until its falsehood was exposed, this fit well
with the story conservatives were trying to spread about Obama's
purported education at the hands of anti-U.S. Muslims.

This is the frontier of Orwellian deception. It makes use of
the way networks of association work, and it makes use of the
fact that the most powerful networks use a combination of
words, images, sounds, and analogies. The only way to combat
twenty-first-century Newspeak is to understand it—and to call
its users on what they are doing every time they do it. Using
language and imagery in a deceptive way is a character issue,
and candidates who fail to call their opponents on it do so at
their—and our—peril. The contemporary purveyors of
Newspeak need to know that Big Brother—or at least the
opposition—is watching them.

Stellar Spin

Frances FitzGerald

I
n May 1983, Ronald Reagan gave another speech about the
growing might of the Soviet nuclear arsenal, Soviet aggression around the world, and the need for more U.S. military
spending. He had delivered the same message so often during
the first two years of his presidency that Defense Department
officials, who had prepared the text, dubbed it "the standard
threat speech." But this time Reagan ended with a few paragraphs of his own. "What," he asked, "if free people could live
secure in the knowledge that their security did not rest upon the
threat of instant U.S. retaliation to deter a Soviet attack; that we
could intercept and destroy strategic ballistic missiles before
they reach our own soil, or that of our allies?" After careful con-
sultation with his advisers, he had, he said, decided to embark
upon a comprehensive effort to create a defense against ballistic
missiles. He acknowledged that the task would be formidable,
and that defenses "if paired with offensive systems," could be
"viewed as fostering an aggressive policy." But with these considerations in mind, he said, "I call upon the scientific community in our country, those who gave us nuclear weapons, to turn
their great talents now to the cause of mankind and world

peace: to give us the means to render these nuclear weapons impotent and obsolete."

The proposal, which had been closely held by a few in the White House, astonished the Joint Chiefs of Staff, Secretary of State George Shultz, and almost everyone else in the national security bureaucracy. Defense Secretary Caspar Weinberger was abroad, but Shultz, who, like Weinberger, had been given a draft of the speech insert just two days before, had pleaded with Reagan not to make it. The technology, Shultz argued, just wasn't there, yet the proposal entailed a revolution in the strategic doctrine of the United States; it ignored U.S. commitments to the Soviet Union under the Anti-Ballistic Missile Treaty, and it would cause a furor among U.S. allies in Europe. Shultz persuaded Reagan to modify the draft—which had apparently promised a fortress America, shielded from all nuclear weapons—but neither he nor Weinberger's deputies could stop him from making his proposal.

In the days after the speech, Democrats in Congress derided the idea as science fiction, and because space weapons were mentioned in background briefings and Reagan had called the Soviet Union "the evil empire," two weeks before, they dubbed the proposal "Star Wars." Editorialists around the country called it everything from a fantasy to a bid for a dangerous new weapons system to a transparent hoax, and defense experts within the administration suggested that the president might have gotten the idea from the movies. White House officials, including Reagan himself, then beat a public retreat, claiming that the initiative entailed nothing more than an extension of the research into anti-missile technologies that had been going on since 1947. Journalists therefore dropped the subject, and for a while nothing more was heard of it.

Yet two years later, Reagan's call for a defense against intercontinental ballistic missiles had, with the backing of Shultz, Weinberger, and every defense expert in the administration, turned into the largest military research program the nation had ever undertaken. In congressional hearings of 1985, Lieutenant General James A. Abrahamson Jr., the director of the newly formed Strategic Defense Initiative Organization (SDIO), asked for $26 billion over five years to fund an array of technologies, including lasers and particle beams, that, he said, could be developed into weapons and integrated into a system to counter the entire Soviet ICBM fleet. The program has continued ever since, but after twenty-two years and an expenditure of over $100 billion, the United States still has no reliable defense against even one long-range ballistic missile, and at the current rate of progress, the country may not have one for the next half century.

How to explain this fantastical endeavor? Certainly it couldn't have come into being without Ronald Reagan, a politician in touch with many quintessential American dreams. But Reagan did not create the program alone. He had help from people with other agendas, and some of these agendas have sustained the program ever since and led to the deployment of a system that has never been operationally tested.

Reagan made his Star Wars speech in a period of intense American anxiety about nuclear war. On taking office, his administration had launched the largest peacetime military buildup in U.S. history. His Defense Department appointees engaged in a great deal of frightening talk about the vulnerability of the U.S. nuclear deterrent and—alternately—their plans to "prevail" in a nuclear war. Believing that only military superiority could make America secure, they had, in addition, blocked all avenues to arms control and almost all contacts with Soviet officials. Their hard-line policies soon gave rise to a powerful grassroots anti-nuclear movement that coalesced around a proposal to freeze both U.S. and Soviet arsenals. The Freeze, as it was called, mobilized millions of people across the country, and by 1983, it was threatening not just the military buildup but Reagan's prospects for reelection. The Star Wars speech was Reagan's first effort to diffuse popular anxiety, and when it failed for lack of support, he turned to more conventional means.

During the election year of 1984, Reagan dropped the threat speech, assured the public that the U.S. deterrent had been restored, and vowed to build a "constructive" relationship with the Soviet Union to reduce the level of arms. That year he spoke often of his "dream" of seeing nuclear weapons banished from the earth. By November, the Freeze had melted away, and thanks in part to a major economic recovery, he won reelection in a landslide.

By that time, the Defense Department had quietly launched the Strategic Defense Initiative (SDI), and when the first major appropriations bill went to the Congress in 1985, administration officials, including those who had been most appalled by Reagan's speech, lined up to testify for it. The mass conversion had nothing to do with the science involved. Rather, top officials at State and Defense had noticed that the Soviets feared that the United States intended to build space weaponry, and they had found other uses for the fledgling program. For Secretary Shultz, SDI was to be a bargaining chip: an inducement to the Soviets to make deep reductions in their nuclear arms in return for weapons that hadn't been invented—"the sleeves off our vest," as he later put it to Reagan. For Secretary Weinberger and his international policy deputy, Richard Perle, SDI was, on the contrary, to be the ultimate weapon against arms control. By then, all administration officials had learned from the polls what Reagan knew instinctively: that SDI, if properly advertised, would prove extremely popular with the American public.

Ever since the 1950s, Americans had told pollsters that they wanted a defense against nuclear weapons and that they were confident that American science could create one. Indeed, when asked, they consistently said that the United States had such a defense already—except when the lack of one was in the news. In other words, Americans were normally in denial about the vulnerability of the country to nuclear destruction, and when they weren't, they trusted that science would make the unthinkable threat disappear. Thus, when Reagan proposed to make nuclear weapons "impotent and obsolete," he was running no risk of raising public incredulity. In fact, a poll taken for the White House two weeks after his speech showed that only one in three Americans doubted that American scientists could come up with "a really effective way to destroy nuclear weapons from space." In 1983, many Americans had worried that Reagan was proposing yet another weapons system, but when he coupled the proposal with promises of arms control and disarmament, his initiative became extremely popular.

There followed a surreal period in U.S. congressional history. While Reagan spoke of a "shield against nuclear weapons" that would protect the country as a roof protects a family from the rain, SDIO officials described ground-based interceptors, space-based battle stations, orbiting mirrors, electromagnetic rail guns, and battle-management computers. They spoke of a multilayered system that could attack Soviet ballistic missiles and warheads in all phases of their flight and produced diagrams showing how this system would work for newspapers and television. Scientists and defense experts from outside the administration objected that the SDIO had seriously underestimated the task of destroying 1,000 or more Soviet ICBMs, each carrying ten or more independently targeted warheads and a cloud of decoys and chaff, in the twenty minutes it took from launch to the descent of their warheads through the atmosphere. Some went into the details of how many battle stations would be needed, their potential vulnerability, and how staggering the costs would be. Others pointed out that the system in all of its complexity would have to be 99.9-percent effective in order to constitute population defenses, for if even 100 Soviet warheads got through, they would destroy 100 American cities. And no weapon, even a rifle, could be relied upon to be 99.9-percent effective. In the hearings, Defense Department experts had to admit that eliminating the threat of ballistic missiles was essentially unachievable, but while Reagan spoke of a "shield" and his officials of "effective defenses," the American public paid no attention to this gloomy arithmetic. Indeed, the fact that distinguished scientists were talking about laser weapons and orbiting battle stations made a space shield sound like near-term possibility.

Over the next three years, Reagan held four summit meetings with Mikhail Gorbachev, the first Soviet president. During this period, Defense and State Department officials waged a series of bureaucratic battles in which Shultz and his deputies attempted to fashion proposals that would result in agreements favorable to the United States, while Weinberger and Perle sought to make all proposals completely unacceptable to the Soviets—and in addition to scrap the ABM Treaty, with the argument that it restricted SDI. At Reykjavik, Iceland, in October 1986, Gorbachev surprised the American side by offering deep cuts in strategic weapons in return for an agreement to confine SDI to laboratory testing for the next ten years. This was just what Shultz had been hoping for, but Reagan, who during the meeting proposed the elimination of all nuclear weapons, refused to make any concessions on SDI. He came away without an agreement, but with a reputation for being both a radical disarmer and a president who would stand up to the Soviets. By the end of his second term, Shultz had managed to obtain an agreement on intermediate nuclear forces, and Senate Democrats had saved the ABM Treaty, but Weinberger and his allies had succeeded in blocking an agreement to reduce strategic nuclear arms.

In 1989, just after Reagan left office, the Joint Chiefs of Staff recommended that SDI be returned to the status quo ante of a small research program on futuristic technologies. In his efforts to abrogate the ABM treaty, Weinberger had punctured the myth of a space shield by putting an anti-missile system on a track to deployment—a move that soon revealed that there was no defense to deploy. President George H.W. Bush had no enthusiasm for Reagan's program, and no more did President Bill Clinton, but neither one made the politically fraught decision to do as the Joint Chiefs advised. Instead, they allowed the attempt to produce national missile defenses to continue, though with less funding and lowered expectations: the hope for a system of ground-based interceptors that might protect the United States against the few missiles that might be launched by "rogue states," such as North Korea or Iraq. Over the course of the years, the program became so entrenched in Washington as to be impervious to the failure of one test after another. The public lost interest, but right-wing Republicans in Congress did not; they dreamed of weapons in space, and every time they came into ascendancy, they would press for the deployment of something, anything, to move the program forward. At the turn of the century, they felt their dream had come true.

In the campaign of 2000, George W. Bush called, as Reagan once had, for deep reductions in U.S. strategic weapons and for a multilayered system of sea-, air-, and space-based defenses to protect the United States and its allies. In its first eight months, the administration blocked a series of multilateral arms control agreements and promised to abrogate the ABM Treaty and deploy national missile defenses in 2004. As soon became clear, most of its officials believed, with Weinberger and Perle, that American security lay only in U.S. ability to deploy superior military force. National Security Adviser Condoleezza Rice spoke of arms control as "the old paradigm." Nonproliferation, or efforts to control the spread of nuclear arms through diplomacy, was replaced with counterproliferation, or efforts to stop potential nuclear attacks by military means. One feature of this new strategy was the invasion of Iraq. Another, which went almost unnoticed in the turmoil that followed, was the deployment of ground-based rockets that administration officials claimed could intercept a missile attack from North Korea or Iran. Defensive technologies are hardly more advanced than they were in the mid-1980s, but the deployments permitted the administration to scrap the ABM Treaty in a politically defensible way. At present—July 2007—the administration is enraging President Vladimir Putin of Russia by planning to place elements of an anti-missile system in Poland and the Czech Republic to intercept missiles from Iran that might be directed at the United States. Putin sees the move as yet another American effort to build military bases in Eastern Europe, and given that Iran doesn't have a long-range missile and that the U.S.

interceptor proposed for deployment hasn't been developed, can't be flight tested until 2013, and, of course, may never work, his explanation seems more plausible than that of the Bush administration.

The U.S. National Missile Defense program is a case study in just what George Orwell warned us about: the power of rhetoric over reality. It is the story of the emperor's new clothes. In the annals of military procurement, there has never been anything like it. However, the deceptions involved, and the uses to which they were put, had antecedents in the Cold War discourse about nuclear weapons. From 1947 on, those in Washington who believed in the need to strengthen the U.S. deterrent often claimed that the Soviets were surging ahead and would soon achieve nuclear superiority, if not a war-winning capability. In the mid-1950s, for example, hawkish Democrats warned of a "bomber gap" and in the late 1950s, of a "missile gap." As it turned out, the United States had many more bombers and missiles than the Soviet Union, but few experts dared contradict these powerful Democrats for fear of being labeled weak on defense. By the early 1970s, both sides had deployed enough nuclear weapons to destroy each other's country many times over. Yet the arms race continued on the dubious theory, wrapped in arcane jargon, that the United States or the Soviet Union would gain the ability to target the other's strategic forces and to win a nuclear war in a second, third, or nth strike. Then, as far as the public was concerned, nuclear superiority had become a synecdoche for the national strength—and a psychological compensation for foreign policy reverses.

In the mid-1970s, Pentagon officials warned of a "window of vulnerability," meaning the period before the deployment of a new type of American missile, when the Soviets would in theory be able to destroy American ICBMs on the ground. Their intelligence turned out to be faulty, but Reagan and his defense advisers spoke of this "window" as if it meant a period when the Soviets would have the capacity to destroy all U.S. strategic forces, and, as Reagan put it, "take us with a phone call." Reagan's solution to this problem was a "shield" against nuclear weapons. It didn't exist, but no more did the problem, so in that sense it was the perfect solution.

The story of the emperor's new clothes ends with the emperor walking through the crowded streets of his capital and a child exclaiming that he is naked. With regard to nuclear weapons, we Americans have most often behaved like the rest of the crowd, relying on the experts to tell us what to think and paying no attention ourselves, preferring to deny the realities. In the early 1980s, the Freeze movement made us sit up and take notice. But then Reagan, with his childlike vision of a magical shield, put us back to sleep, and in twenty-two years no one has woken us from our dream of a defense against nuclear weapons.

Bad Knowledge

ALICE O'CONNOR

Knowledge—of the evidence-based variety, anyway—has come in for quite a beating from our avowedly "faith-based" administration and the right-wing political establishment it represents. Hardly a day goes by without some new revelation about otherwise well-vetted social or scientific intelligence having been deliberately suppressed, ignored, or, more likely, preempted by the expertise generated by the nation's conservative policy intelligentsia—invariably for the sake of political advantage but almost always in the name of such higher purposes as God, free markets, heterosexual marriage, and war.

This may strike even the most cynical as singularly hypocritical, what with the mania for standardized testing we've imposed on school-aged children. More chilling is to see its political consequences in the Orwellian twists of law and logic that have brought us warrant-less wiretaps, extraordinary rendition, and official sanction of torture. Still, the assault on knowledge is not something that stirs the kind of political passion that, were he here to witness it, Orwell would have urged us to summon. Indeed, struggles over the integrity of knowledge are considered rather like government oversight or civil service reform: important and well-meaning, but somehow peripheral to the real business of politics, which is more fixated on winning the next election than on bringing rigor and accountability to public discourse.

But the tattered state of knowledge is not simply the work of a rogue administration, nor something that can be repaired by a return to some commonly accepted standards of objectivity, as to a mythical golden age of reason and political consensus. It is a consequence of wider and more historically rooted developments in American political culture that have made knowledge a thing of technocratic think tanks as well as of political and ideological warfare. Orwell didn't know about these developments, which are rooted as much in the politics of Cold War liberal "consensus" as in late twentieth-century conservatism. Nevertheless, we can look to Orwell to understand how these otherwise very different impulses feed off one another in the ongoing proliferation of bad knowledge: the right-wing ideologues by appropriating technocratic tools of inquiry; the neutralized experts by separating "the facts" from the underlying values, social purposes, and historical contexts that give them meaning.

The Orwell I invoke is the author not only of *1984* but of "Politics and the English Language," first published in 1946 and centrally concerned with the deceptively simple task of rooting out the bad habits that were then muddying both academic and political writing. To Orwell, bad writing signaled a more profound break between words and their meaning, and from there the prospect of politics reduced to propaganda—he singled out words that certainly resonate with our current situation, such as *democracy,* and *freedom.* I offer here a highly abbreviated facsimile of that essay's memorable exercise in textual exegesis, with the aim of making a parallel point: that bringing clarity and meaning to the values and thinking that shape our understanding of "the facts" is no peripheral matter. It is the first step toward recovering political principles that, thanks in no small part to what conservative movement ideologues trumpet as a "war of ideas," have been distorted in "defense of the indefensible," to quote Orwell's all-too-appropriate phrase.

The passages excerpted below offer examples of authoritative knowledge as it is now routinely purveyed in decision-making circles, which is to say, in the neutralized language of policy analysis and under the auspices of research institutes and think tanks that claim to hold themselves above the political fray. In fact, these passages come to us in some fashion from the leading idea mills of the right, prominent among which are the multi-issue Heritage Foundation, and the Cato, American Enterprise, and Manhattan Institutes, and the more "family-values"–focused Family Research Council. Established or significantly refashioned since the 1970s, these and other think tanks have been churning out "research" ever since, in a thinly veiled campaign to promote free market economics, limited government, and their version of "traditional" morality. Backstopping their efforts has been a steady investment of right-wing philanthropic and private-donor contributions. This philanthropic venture capital has in turn spawned a remarkable proliferation of similarly intentioned institutions that have taken the knowledge crusade to the state and local level while cultivating "experts" in the fields of law, city planning, and lately in the environmental and biological sciences. That they have succeeded by mimicking the institutional apparatus and modus operandi of the so-called liberal establishment is but one indication of their self-designated role as a conservative "counterintelligentsia," with all the reverberations of counterrevolutionary vanguardism that term invokes. In playing out this role, they have thus far managed to negotiate the significant internal differences and tensions within the movement, in part by demonizing liberalism as an overarching threat to "traditional" values, whether of family, freedom, or property rights.

The passages I've chosen touch on issues that have been on the front lines of the "culture wars" for more than three decades, but that is not my main purpose in singling them out. Equally important, they share two commonalities. They are statements of moral or ideological conviction reported in the conventions of social scientific and historical inquiry. They are also highly misleading and in some cases demonstrably false.

1. An article in the *Journal of the American Medical Association* by Dr. Michael Resnick and others entitled "Protecting Adolescents from Harm: Findings from the National Longitudinal Study on Adolescent Health" shows that "abstinence pledge" programs are dramatically effective in reducing sexual activity among teenagers in grades 7 through 12. Based on a large national sample of adolescents, the study concludes that "Adolescents who reported having taken a pledge to remain a virgin were at significantly lower risk of early age of sexual debut." In fact, the study found that participating in an abstinence program and taking a formal pledge of virginity were by far the most significant factors in a youth's delaying early sexual activity.... [T]he authors discovered that the level of sexual activity among students who had taken a formal

pledge of virginity was one-fourth the level of that of their counterparts who had not taken a pledge.

—**Robert Rector,** *Heritage Foundation Backgrounder on Abstinence Education,* 2002.

2. If Americans are serious about making major inroads on illegitimacy, the most important unanswered policy question is this: What would be the effect of eliminating welfare for unmarried mothers altogether . . . ? The present ability to estimate the effect is severely limited. Suppose for purposes of argument that a percentage point reduction in the welfare package is associated with a half percentage point reduction in the nonmarital birthrate (a magnitude consistent with the set of studies finding a substantial relationship). The observed values of changes in benefits in the real world that produce these estimates are highly truncated, usually representing a small percentage of the value of the welfare package. They provide no adequate basis for assessing whether the observed effect would be linear across the range. . . . The point is that people do not know, and cannot know, what the real shape of the reductions in fertility might be across the whole range of reductions in the welfare package unless some state cuts off all benefits (or something approaching that ideal) to some subset of women. A plausible test case would be for a state with a relatively small caseload and a history of effective nongovernmental social welfare—the Western plains and mountain states offer several possibilities—to cut off all benefits for girls under the age of 21.

—**Charles Murray,** in a Brookings Institution volume entitled *The New World of Welfare,* 2001.

3. For comparative purposes, the net warming of the twentieth century is approximately 0.8 C. . . . That warming was clearly accompanied by a dramatic improvement in health and welfare, with life expectancies rising more than 60 percent and per capita income, in constant dollars, increasing tenfold in the United States. Given that 1.8 C is a more plausible projection of warming over the next century, because it reconciles models and observations, it is difficult to defend the notion that carbon dioxide is a pollutant requiring immediate remediation under the Clean Air Act. . . . Because of the facts, and the lack of any comprehensive assessment of the risks and benefits of greenhouse gas emissions and regulation, it is simply impossible to conclude that the net effect of greenhouse gases is an endangerment of health and welfare.

—Amicus brief submitted by the Competitive Enterprise Institute in *Commonwealth of Massachusetts v.*
U.S. Environmental Protection Agency, 2006.

4. The index published in *Economic Freedom of the World* measures the degree to which the policies and institutions of countries are supportive of economic freedom. The cornerstones of economic freedom are personal choice, voluntary exchange, freedom to compete, and security of privately owned property. Thirty-eight data points are used to construct a summary index and to measure the degree of economic freedom in five areas: (1) size of government; (2) legal structure and security of property rights; (3) access to sound money; (4) freedom to trade

internationally; and (5) regulation of credit, labour, and business.

—Executive summary, *Economic Freedom of the World: 2006 Annual Report,* co-published by The Cato Institute and the Simon Fraser Institute.

5. The courts began the process of reviving racial classification in schools by ignoring the distinction (which Martin Luther King, Jr. understood) between desegregation and integration. Desegregation is a restriction on government power. The state may not use race as the basis for school assignments. Desegregation permits racial separation as long as it is not compelled by government. Integration, by contrast, is a state-mandated result. The government overrides personal and parental choices in order to make sure that different racial groups get the same education and obtain it together.

—Dinesh D'Souza, *The End of Racism,* 1995

These are hardly the only or most provocative examples I could have chosen. I have deliberately skipped over any number of authoritative-sounding pronouncements about the absence of "sound science" on global warming, or on the merits of Charles Darwin versus "intelligent design." I have also left out a good deal of statistical doublespeak about how, in the United States, poor people aren't really poor (they have air-conditioning and own color TVs) and wouldn't be poor in any case if only they would work more, get married, and have fewer children. Instead, the examples I have chosen display a handful of what

Orwell might have called the "verbal tics" and "mental vices" common not just to conservatives but to the wider knowledge industry—bad habits through which intelligence is made to seem innocuous or otherwise disconnected from consideration of its political meaning. Thus, even as they report *mis*information about a gamut of politically charged issues from abstinence-only education to economic regulation and school integration, the statements quoted above take advantage of characteristic weaknesses in the apparatus of expert inquiry to make it appear as if profound differences in morality and political philosophy were merely differences of interpretation and fact. Setting aside the sheer dullness of the language, these weaknesses include, but are no means confined to:

1. *Hidden premises.* The passages I've quoted are couched in empiricist terms, even as they advance moral or ideological premises. While ostensibly grounding their conclusions in the narrow logic of the data (or its absence), their value premises are built in as elements of research methodology or in the formulation of the questions. Thus, in the course of reporting (erroneously) that virginity pledges delay teenage "sexual debut," Robert Rector (1) depicts sexual activity as "harm" and abstinence as the only acceptable protection. Charles Murray's logic (2) rests on the proposition that reducing "illegitimacy" and promoting heterosexual marriage are the most urgent priorities of welfare reform. Dinesh D'Souza (5) manages to equate court-mandated integration with Jim Crow segregation, based on definitions drawn from doctrinaire anti-statism. Of course, value premises creep into even the most arduously "neutral" analysis, where they are even less likely

to be acknowledged. The point is that in either instance, the value premises are effectively taken off the table as legitimate subjects for scrutiny and debate, only to become absorbed as the unexamined assumptions and points of "consensus" that frame the larger policy conversation.

2. *Misleading "indicators."* The passages I've quoted deploy several commonly used devices for making the abstract and normative artificially measurable and concrete: Rector (1) and Murray (2) use what are generally referred to as sexual and reproductive "outcomes" to gauge traditional virtue; a group of analysts affiliated with the Competitive Enterprise Institute (3) weigh in on behalf of economic gain over environmental regulation based on spurious cost-benefit trade-offs; the libertarian Cato and Simon Fraser Institutes (4) translate their decidedly market-friendly definition of economic "freedom" into a compilation of "data points." And yet, in the give-and-take of quantified policy analysis, it is the measures that take on the greater air of reality and become the currency of discussion, rather than the norms and assumptions they indirectly promote. Once tied to a set of measurable "outcomes," the debate over abstinence-only education is about whether it "works" rather than about whether the state should be enforcing the moral worldview it promotes. A similar point can be made about the measurable outcomes (e.g., child welfare) that liberals use to justify such broader objectives as the equitable distribution of income or an expanded vision of public goods. The problem is not that the indicators are less worthy of discussion so much as that they are used to

obscure rather than to illuminate a more meaningful political conversation.

3. *Methodological creep.* The methodological imperatives that dominate the knowledge industry—for statistical accuracy, comparability, evaluation, or the longed-for "gold standard" known as experimental design—can become the blunting instruments that make even the most incendiary ideological propositions seem reasoned "options" in the quest for better policy. No one has mastered this art better than Charles Murray, revered on the right as the author of the extended "thought experiment" *(Losing Ground)* that helped to end welfare, and quoted above (2) offering up an experiment in Malthusian morality to answer an "unanswered policy question." And yet, in the ideologically neutered world of welfare evaluation, Murray's proposals are effectively exempted from ideological scrutiny, treated as possibly extreme but basically as methodological matters. This in turn serves as a peculiar form of validation, as these and other once impossibly radical proposals are made to seem plausible once "operationalized" within the channels of policy analysis.

4. *Pretentious diction.* Orwell used this term when writing about words that "give an air of scientific impartiality to biased judgments," in an observation that could just as readily be applied to the use of phrases (e.g., "national sample," "observed effect," "plausible projection," "measures the degree") deployed in these passages from the right. Certainly, the language is less moralized and more tempered than the analyses and policy positions it describes. But the

hyper-scientized idiom of expertise is also insulating and inaccessible to outsiders and for that reason can be used as a buffer against fully public accountability. Most people have no way of knowing, for example, that the "99.9 percent confidence level" the Heritage Foundation reported for abstinence evaluations was based on statistically biased samples and other suspect measures. Of course, one could conclude that this is precisely why we need experts to keep the charlatans in check, but that only caves in to the aura of authority conveyed by needless opacity.

5. *Historical vacuums.* Of all the weaknesses in policy analysis, none has played more to right-wing advantage than the neglect of history and a more general resistance to historical ways of thinking. Only in a universe in which history is ignored does economic growth become the "benefit" of environmental pollution (3), the absence of labor regulation and property-rights restrictions a measurement of economic "freedom," (4) and Martin Luther King and the *Brown v. Board of Education* decision the vehicles for upholding a rigidly "color-blind" constitutionalism (5). Left unexamined are not only the misleading facts and points of interpretation, but also the deeply distorted historical narratives—about our mythically individualistic, "laissez-faire" past as much as about the permissive decadence of "big government" liberalism—that have become absorbed into the dominant political culture. Such narratives have been reduced to relentlessly repeated slogans, but their flattened view of history has been of consequence as the analytic backdrop for a series of radical reforms.

That the right-wing intelligentsia has used the analytic apparatus of the knowledge industry to its advantage is of course but a small part of its success in promoting conservative values and ideology. The larger story is grounded much more deeply in the politics that fueled the right-wing conservative ascendancy. It reminds us that the culture wars that conservatives launched to such great effect in the 1970s and 1980s were not just about sex and family values and moral declension. They were about what we know and how we know it, and about who should control the terms of the social conversation as well as the boundaries of political possibility.

But as Orwell might have noted, the rise of the faith-based intelligentsia raises the uncomfortable possibility that even those who have been most alarmed about the assault on knowledge have been somehow, if inadvertently, complicit. Repairing the damage, in turn, requires looking beyond the right's cynical manipulation of research findings. It means changing the habits of thought in the broader political culture, habits that have made it easier to use the disembodied facts and tools of inquiry to obscure political meaning, ironically by failing to acknowledge the legitimate relationship between objective fact and social valuation.

So I will close by suggesting a few simple guidelines for weeding out the bad habits along with the bad science, ultimately in the interest of promoting political knowledge that is at once empirically rigorous, understandable, and clear about its values and social purposes.

1. Never trust statements of faith or ideological doctrine when presented as scientific fact.

2. Be equally skeptical of claims to ideological neutrality, especially those that skirt or ignore ideology.

3. Before giving credence to measurable outcomes and indicators, find out what they measure, who is doing the measuring, and why.

4. Never accept findings stripped of social and historical context, especially for the sake of narrow principle or statistical precision.

5. Resist the temptation to defer to the authority of scientific jargon—or to studies that report a confidence level of 99.9 percent.

As Orwell noted in a very different but parallel context, guidelines such as these are elementary, but they also invite deeper changes. They invite changes in the attitudes and practices that get in the way of the kind of inquiry that restores meaning to concepts such as "democracy" and "freedom." Above all, to echo Orwell, they invite greater clarity about ideas that do not always lend themselves to narrow empirical tests.

Black and White, or Gray:
A Polish Conundrum

KONSTANTY GEBERT

G iven the benefit of hindsight, George Orwell can be accused of a certain naïveté. A merciless critic of total-itarian propaganda, he seemed to believe that a demo-cratic system was basically immune to it—not because democratic leaders are necessarily any better, but because the system itself, with its polyphony of voices, does not lend itself to a monopoly of Newspeak. "In our time"—he wrote in his mas-terful "Politics and the English Language"—"it is broadly true that political writing is bad writing. Where it is not true, it will generally be found that the writer is some kind of rebel, ex-pressing his private opinions and not a 'party line.' Orthodoxy, of whatever color, seems to demand a lifeless, imitative style."

ORWELL WAS RIGHT—but he did not foresee a time when democracy itself, not only Big Brother, would replace writing with telescreens. Bad writing makes for good TV: Cutting sound bites, and incisive images, have a persuasive power against which the rebels Orwell mentions are remarkably powerless. When political discourse is conducted on government-controlled TV, no amount of scribblings can counter the impact of the image or the selected quote. The government no longer needs to control the scribblers. Their very existence, once they are either safely removed from the telescreens or, if present there, neutered by the nature of the telescreens' discourse, seemingly disproves accusations that free debate has been stifled.

Nowhere are these lessons more apparent than in Poland, a country that made a successful transition to parliamentary democracy after a half century of Totalitarianism, but where "Orwellian" tendencies have hung on tenaciously. No, Poland is not about to revert to political practices of the past. But Orwell would have immediately recognized the language of political discourse as practiced there today.

Polish politics since 1989 have been messy and confusing, as democratic politics often are. Still, political discourse in Poland after that seemed to have steered largely clear of the outright corruption of public discourse, demagoguery, and witch hunts, infamously associated with Communism. But in the fall of 2005, things changed when a right-wing party—Law and Justice—won both the parliamentary and presidential elections and mounted against its adversaries a campaign of unprecedented brutality. Its leaders, however, clearly did not see it that way.

When in 1989 we recovered independence, the liberal current was dominant in the world and in part in Poland also. The Polish version of liberalism proved to be very useful to the Communist nomenclature defending its interests. It proved useful also to those who feared the revitalization of genuine political traditions in Poland, and who, though they had been active in Solidarity with great merit, also had the ambition for the new Poland to be their

Poland, and only theirs. Ruled only by them. This is how the al-
liance of rejection of the Solidarity tradition was created. A post-
Communist monster was built in Poland. . . . This is why we have
created a difficult but logical coalition. The coalition of those who
are against the system.[1]

The man speaking these words is not an extremist agitator,
haranguing the crowds in the early days of Poland's post-
Communist transformation, but one of the architects of that
transformation, a politician respected for his oppositionist
past.[2] The year is 2006, seventeen years after "the system" was
peacefully overthrown, and the speaker, Jarosław Kaczyński, is
the chairman of the country's strongest political party and
prime minister of the coalition government it created. His twin
brother, Lech Kaczyński, is now the country's president.[3] They
have been in power for more than a year. If there is a "post-
Communist monster" in Poland, they are among those who
created it, and are now running it. And yet Jarosław Kaczyński
speaks as the leader of "the coalition of those who are against
the system."

And it is a strange coalition. Its main force is the twin brothers' Law and Justice Party, which scored a plurality in the parliamentary elections of 2005, running against an incumbent
post-Communist government deeply mired in corruption and
abuse of power. It campaigned on a platform opposed both to
the post-Communists and to the liberalism of the other main
opposition party, the center-right Civic Platform—yet it had
promised it would govern in a coalition with the liberals.
When, however, the extent of its electoral victory became clear
(the other Kaczyński won the election for president)—it turned
against its partners-to-be with disdain. Coalition talks came to

naught, and after a brief period of minority government, Law and Justice settled for a coalition deal with two smaller parties: Self-Defense and the League of Polish Families.

While both Law and Justice and Civic Platform can legitimately claim to be heirs to different strands of the Solidarity tradition, this can hardly be said of the ruling party's coalition partners. Self-Defense is a peasant movement, created out of a populist revolt against paying bank credits. Its leader, Andrzej Lepper, currently a deputy prime minister and minister of agriculture, and former member of the Communist Party, carries an infamous reputation: He was accused in Polish *Newsweek* of beating up the prostitutes he brings to his party headquarters, has been sentenced six times for slander, and has dozens of cases pending for different criminal offenses, as do leading activists of the party (his former right-hand man is currently under investigation for rape). Is this really the man Jarosław Kaczyński would freely choose as his partner to undertake his declared "moral revolution?"[4] The leader of Law and Justice had not always been so enthusiastic about Self-Defense. Before the elections, he stated that the party "had been set up by officers of the former [Communist] security service,"[5] while he later said of Lepper himself that he "has shown his disdain for the law, and that he is a political wrecker. The support of Law and Justice for this politician in any situation is out of the question."[6] In the summer of 2007, in a surprise move, prime minister Kaczyński fired Lepper, who found himself under investigation for corruption. Lepper had already been fired from the government once before, in 2006, by Kaczyński—only to return. But without Lepper's party, Law and Justice does not have a majority in Parliament. Throughout the summer, politicians from both the major and junior coalition parties played brinkmanship games, trying to avoid early elections with the fear that all three would lose, while at the same time attempting to blackmail each other into accepting their different political demands. "This is not about ideological principles. This is about political power," League leader Wojciech Wierzejski commented candidly.

The second coalition party, the extreme-right League of Polish Families, led by Roman Giertych, who is currently a deputy prime minister and the minister of education, also seems an odd bedfellow for someone who had promised to "complete the Solidarity revolution." The father of the League's leader, professor Maciej Giertych, had under martial law been an adviser to General Wojciech Jaruzelski; his son—too young himself to have participated in the Solidarity movement—had never distanced himself from his father's politics, even though Giertych senior remains a main adviser both to his son and to the League. The idea of Law and Justice allying itself with either Self-Defense or the League originally seemed outlandish to Kaczyński as well. In the fall of 2005, when coalition negotiations with Civic Platform were still underway, a radio journalist asked Kaczyński what he thought about a possible government with himself as prime minister, Giertych as deputy prime minister, and Lepper as minister of agriculture. "This shows how aggravated our colleagues [from Civic Platform] are," replied Kaczyński, clearly suggesting that the very idea was disinformation. "They know perfectly well that such a government cannot be created."[7] Nine months later it was a fact.

Lepper might be a thug and Giertych an extremist—but both were desirable allies in the struggle against "the system." That "post-Communist monster" was composed, in Kaczyński's words, of the former Communists and their allies from the former opposition, former secret police agents, and shady business interests, tainted by mafia connections and foreign influences. It emphatically did not include a party supposedly set up by former agents, nor one that followed the teachings of a former Jaruzelski adviser, nor, indeed, the twin brothers themselves—but it clearly could include some of the major figures of the anti-Communist opposition, if they were critical of the "anti-system" crusade. Such was the fate, for instance, of Adam Michnik, who had spent twenty years in the opposition (six of these in jail) and was one of the prime figures of Poland's democratic transformation and subsequent political life.

The confrontation erupted when the editor in chief of *Gazeta Wyborcza* attacked Kaczyński's "lustration" program. Lustration, or vetting, was to be a main instrument of struggle against "the system." It involved demanding that persons "holding positions or exercising professions of public trust" make legal statements about whether in the past they had or had not been agents or informers of Communist secret services. Those who admitted to such activity, as well as those whom the government considered to have lied on their statement and those who refused to submit one, would lose the right to hold the said position or exercise the said profession for ten years. The statements would be verified against former secret police files, now in government custody; the government would also publish a "list of agents." If someone considered his name had been wrongly placed on such a list, he could sue the government—but the burden of proof would be on him. All the government had to prove was that secret police evidence of guilt exists.

The lustration law was extraordinary not only because it was passed in 2006, seventeen years after the fall of Communism, and abolished the presumption of innocence and imposed collective responsibility, but also because of its scope: It covered not only all persons exercising elective or appointed political positions but entire professions, such as journalism and university teaching; some 700,000 people were affected. Finally, it did not allow for distortions and forgeries in the secret police files, which were treated as a font of absolute truth, even though previous cases, under an earlier, more civilized lustration law, including one involving a deputy prime minister in the Kaczyński government, Zyta Gilowska (and another involving Kaczyński himself), had shown that files had, in fact, been forged. The professions rebelled,[8] and *Gazeta* supported them. Eventually, the constitutional court threw most of the lustration law out. The president's reaction was to state that the court itself was suspect—and that its judges should be investigated, together with their family members.

Journalists were supposedly particularly tainted. "A huge group of people making up today's media market is compromised. This will become completely clear when the files will be opened. None of the so-called opinion-making media in Poland is free of participation in these activities,"[9] said the prime minister. Intellectuals—in Parliament he called them the "mendacious elites"[10]—did not fare much better, though Kaczyński attempted to limit his attack: "Yes, we are critical, even very critical, of a group of merely several hundred, which finds itself in many important points of our social life, sometimes endowed with different titles, lives in a closed world, mainly among their own, and among its own convinces itself of its being right, and of the savagery of everybody else."[11]

This was his only contribution to the debate that had been conducted on the pages of newspapers. State TV, which is government controlled, did not give sufficient airtime to the government's critics and often misquoted them. State radio purged itself entirely of those who refused to endorse lustration. But state TV did not even need to. With precious few job openings in private TV, its employees were very careful not to fall from grace. And just to make sure, private TV was tarred with the same brush as the "mendacious elites"—labeled as part of the same conspiracy that works to thwart the truth.

ADAM MICHNIK had consistently criticized lustration, ever since the first attempts at introducing it in the 1990s; as late as last year, he called it "the omnipotent rule of a nightmare police of memory and blackmail"[12]—though eventually he became convinced that leaks, which had already smeared a number of public figures, cannot be stopped, so he decided to support the idea of simply opening the files to all. Kaczyński, commenting on Michnik's position, responded, "Yes, he did spend six years in Communist prisons, but what did he fight for? In a nutshell: Did he fight for independent Poland, or for the victory of the Puławianie [liberal Communists] over Natolin [dogmatic Communists]? This is a question which, in the light of his activity over at least the last eighteen years, has to be answered." And the prime minister concluded: "He is in essence a man of the same formation as the [post-Communist] SLD [Sojusz Lewicy Demokratycznej]."[13] This was hardly Kaczyński's first attack on *Gazeta:* He had already accused Helena Łuczywo, deputy editor in chief of *Gazeta Wyborcza* daily (Michnik is the editor in chief) and veteran underground activist, of both "being of Communist Party of Poland provenience [origin]" and of "directing Civic Platform"[14]—this after Łuczywo had commented positively on recent Civic Platform policies. In general,

Gazeta Wyborcza is to the prime minister "a late, mutated form of the Communist Party of Poland," and in his opinion, "the weaker *Gazeta* is, the better it is for Poland."[15]

Even for a politician not known for his verbal moderation, such accusations are surprising. The Communist Party of Poland (KPP) was dissolved by Stalin years before either Michnik or Łuczywo were born, and neither had been a member of its postwar avatar, the Polish United Workers Party (PZPR). And yet, as Kaczyński explained, this hardly matters, for their parents had both belonged to the KPP:

> If one person had a father, and maybe even a mother in the KPP, and is active in a milieu—he explained—and such people exist also on the Right [a veiled reference to his closest collaborator Ludwik Dorn], this is irrelevant. But if there exists an entire milieu in which practically everybody had parents in the KPP, and furthermore these people have a powerful instrument of influencing the consciousness of the Poles, we have a problem. Especially given that on the pages of this powerful instrument some KPP ideas . . . are being continued. The radical questioning of national values is an element of this continuation.[16]

In fact, some editors and journalists of *Gazeta*, myself included, had parents who were KPP or PZPR members.[17] This might have accounted for our decision to join the anti-Communist underground, but hardly for political choices made after 1989—unless the prime minister meant to imply that Communist affiliation of the parents is a flaw that determines children's political behavior. The other possibility would be that by "Communists" he meant "Jews," as suggested by his remark about "national values." This interpretation is implausible, however, in the light of the twin brothers' consistent and unquestionable opposition to anti-Semitism;[18] in fact, in the government's political language, homosexuals play the role traditionally ascribed to Jews, as a danger to the nation and a source of moral decay.[19]

Jarosław Kaczyński's twin brother, Lech, Poland's president, seems to share his obsession about Communist parents. Commenting on the court ruling mentioned earlier, in which Zyta Gilowska was absolved of accusations of having been an informer, Lech Kaczyński said: "I know what milieu judge Mojkowska [who made the ruling] comes from. This should not have any importance, but yesterday [when the ruling was issued] I lost that certainty." And his brother supported him: "There are situations in which the truth must be told," he added.[20]

This obsession is not limited to Communists, or indeed to parents. During the 2005 presidential elections, Jarosław Kurski, chief spin doctor for Law and Justice, had falsely accused Donald Tusk of Civic Platform, Lech Kaczyński 's major and ultimately defeated rival for the presidency, of having had a grandfather who had volunteered for the Wehrmacht during World War II.[21] The accusation was consistent with the Kaczyńskis' anti-German phobias, second only to their anti-Communist and anti-gay ones. Kurski was fully aware of having lied, but he was sure the lie would cost Tusk votes. "This Wehrmacht thing is bogus, but we're riding it, for the dumb masses will buy it,"[22] he candidly confided to fellow journalists. Briefly expelled from Law and Justice, he soon returned to prominence. After a TV debate between the candidates, Tusk asked Kaczyński: "Why do you keep this SOB?" "He might be an SOB, but I prefer to have him on my side," replied the future president.

In essence, therefore, having allied himself with a party he suspects of having been set up by former Communist agents and run by a former Communist party member, and another that follows the teachings of a former adviser to general Jaruzelski, Jarosław Kaczyński started a crusade to destroy the "post-Communist monster," a creature made up of former Communists, their children, suspected lackeys of foreign powers and their grandchildren, journalists, academics—in fact everyone but himself and his allies. On the face of it, this strategy seems bizarre and counterproductive, for it is sure to make enemies and seems to produce no friends.

And yet this is a well-considered strategy and may yet prove successful. Kaczyński is making a consistent appeal to Poland's "silent majority," which had supported neither the Communist regime nor the opposition, for it was sure both would ultimately be defeated. Since 1989, this silent majority has been living with a bitter taste in its mouth, because the opposition emerged victorious. Kaczyński, determining by fiat who is and who is not an anti-Communist, makes it possible for them to get a certificate of civic virtue after the fact, merely by granting him their support. At a pro-government rally organized by Solidarity, he put it succinctly: "We are where we were then; they [the critics of the government] are where the riot police were."[23] By attacking former underground legends such as Adam Michnik as de facto Communists, he legitimizes the silent majority's choice to deny them their support. By enrolling former Communists on his side, he makes it possible for the silent majority to feel finally free of guilt for having supported oppression.[24] It seems certain he sees nothing wrong in all this. "There is only good in me,"[25] he confided to a *Gazeta Wyborcza* reporter. And certainly the silent majority is a bigger electorate than the "mendacious elites" he crusades against.

As George Orwell wrote in "Politics and the English Language":

> When one critic writes, "The outstanding feature of Mr. X's work is its living quality," while another writes, "The immediately striking thing about Mr. X's work is its peculiar deadness," the reader accepts this as a simple difference of opinion. If words like *black* and *white* were involved, instead of the jargon words *dead* and *living*, he would see at once that language was being used in an improper way.

Little did he know.

When, in his parliamentary exposé,[26] Jarosław Kaczyński said: "No cries and no lamentations will convince us that white is white and black is black," I genuinely (for a moment) thought he had made a slip of the tongue.

After the Falwellians

Susan Harding

Professional reticence prevented me from calling the churchpeople of the Reverend Jerry Falwell "Falwellians" when I wrote a book about them some years ago. It seemed like a cheap shot at the time, but, looking back, it seems like a chance missed. The allusion to George Orwell was well worth pursuing.

Now that Jerry Falwell, having already passed his prime, is dead and buried, perhaps it is time to ask: What would Orwell say?

Falwell would most definitely not have fared well if Orwell had been able to examine his language by the standards established in his famous essay "Politics and the English Language." Falwell's language was riddled with the "stale or mixed images," the "prefabricated phrases, needless repetitions, and humbug and vagueness generally" that Orwell deplored.[1] But what if Orwell had decided he needed a more robust view of language, having come to the conclusion that idealizing language as a tool of logic and transparent communication was too limiting? What if, instead of evaluating Falwell on the basis of linguistic precision, the criterion were cultural efficacy? What did Falwell, his churchpeople, and the religious right more generally do to their language and to ours that changed them and us?

In the 1980s and 1990s, the Falwellians built the first modern fundamentalist "revoicing" empire.[2] Revoicing practices convert the cultural stuff of others into one's own. Falwell's church ministries, media and political organizations, and educational institutions were, in effect, a hive of cultural workshops in which both fundamentalist and secular ideas, images, narratives, and practices were smelted, refashioned, melded, packaged, and distributed with spectacular success.

The Falwellians converted the demon-friendly haunted house of Halloween into Scaremare, an ensemble of creepy encounters with sin, dying, death, and the saving grace of Jesus Christ. They took up the secular beauty contest and turned it into a "pageant" that emphasized Christian virtues more than physical appearance. They published *Fundamentalist Journal,* a glossy news and opinion magazine that staged its world-consuming rhetoric on coffee tables around the county. Jerry Falwell's Bible college, Lynchburg Baptist College, morphed into a liberal arts college, Liberty Baptist College, and then into a university, Liberty University. The Museum of Earth and Life History on its campus occupied the cultural space of a museum of natural history, but recoded the displays of man and beast with the assumptions of creation science rather than evolution. Liberty Godparent Homes converted a former home for unwed mothers into a staging ground for pro-life save-a-baby narratives that in turn revoiced feminist story lines in born-again Christian terms.

Parallel world-consuming industries emerged during those years all over the country in theological conservative Protestant churches, ministries, parachurch organizations, and religious businesses. The end of the twentieth century was a period of born-again Christian cultural diaspora, one of cultural morphing, colonizing, and recoding that left nothing untouched, not even the Bible.

Revolve: The Complete New Testament. The number one reason teens don't read the Bible more is that it's too big and freaky looking. We asked them, "What do you read?" . . . And the answer was, magazines, teen magazines. . . . The Revolve Bible is a Bible that looks like a teen fashion magazine. . . . God isn't in a leather Bible at all times. He not some God in a box, has to come in a leather flex edition. He's all about meeting people where they are. That's what Revolve is.[3]

BibleZines, Christian Bibles published in the form of glossy magazines, show how far the process has gone and that it is not over. *Revolve,* the New Testament for teenage girls, came out first, in 2003, followed shortly by *Real,* the New Testament for urban (which means here multiethnic, edgy, and guy-centered) teens, and *Refuel,* a glossy version of *Revolve* for teenage boys. Tweens, kids, and adults have also now been targeted with their own BibleZines: *Blossom, Magnify, Explore, Divine Health, NT:Sport, Becoming,* and *Align.*

* * *

THESE ARE THE REVOICING practices of an imperial discourse. They redirect, reaccentuate, swerve, reinflect, reinscribe, recode, revalorize, and re-version. Revoicing requires intimate, inside knowledge of the social life of others. It is work done from within their discourses, work that creates unprecedented points of view within the discourses and ventriloquizes and redirects them to other, sometimes entirely opposite, ends.

BibleZines show how sophisticated—glossy, hip, and slick—theologically conservative Christians have become in revoicing "the world" (in this case, through teen magazines, youth culture, niche marketing, and so on) in their own cultural terms. As activists, voters, and lobbyists, Christians who are socially as well as theologically conservative have also transformed the American political landscape. Their ability to revoice and dominate the basic idioms of American politics became dramatically apparent in the presidential elections of 2000 and 2004. During the decades leading up to those elections, leaders of the religious right, as well as Republican politicians and pundits, became adept at rethinking and respeaking their liberal opponents' terms, at reinflecting and redirecting them into their own terms. They did not just criticize or mock their cultural and political adversaries; they metabolized them. They went deep inside hitherto secular and liberal institutions and practices, not to be assimilated but to assimilate, to consume, digest, and convert both the partisan and the cultural politics they encountered to their ends.

The Falwellians went well beyond the kind of linguistic imprecision and manipulation that Orwell condemned. As the linguist Geoffrey Nunberg argued in 2006, the right "captured" the language of the nation's everyday political discussion. "Language is a kind of informal plebiscite: When we adopt a new kind of word or alter the usage of an old one, we're casting a voice vote for a particular point of view. . . . When we talk about politics nowadays—by 'we' I mean progressives and liberals as well as conservatives and people in the center—we can't help using language that embodies the worldview of the right."[4]

Religious right preachers were pioneers in revoicing the language of liberalism. They trained their churchpeople in how to follow suit and created and revamped a network of day schools, colleges, and universities to train growing generations of students in the skills, basic and advanced, of challenging, confronting, and converting the world, its politics as well as its culture, to their terms.[5] They skillfully revoiced liberal ideas, tropes, and story lines about citizenship, government, America, democracy, freedom, liberty, class, family, civil rights, social justice, the Constitution, and peace. In so doing, they provided much of the intellectual ammunition that displaced liberal "reality-based" versions of social policy, political economics, and geopolitics with conservative "faith-based" ones.[6]

One distinct advantage activists of the religious right have over their secular critics and rivals is that although they have no inhibitions about revoicing secular idioms, most of their secular critics and rivals cannot, or will not, revoice conservative religious idioms. Even if they had the insider knowledge that revoicing requires, they willfully gag themselves. Their position is that such idioms have no place in modern public life because they are based on faith, not reason. The only solution is to get rid of them and to reinstate a "naked public square"[7] in which public life is defined as off-limits to all but banal forms of religious speech.

The problem is that such an arrangement depends on everyone playing by a tacit set of rules that restrict religious speech. What do you do when a religiously inspired party, in particular, a party you absolutely disagree with, breaks the taboo? What if that party becomes adept at absorbing and digesting your narrative and rhetorical resources? Unless other parties talk back in ways that absorb and digest the narrative and rhetorical resources of the religiously inspired party, that party's religious idioms may run amok and unopposed through the body politic. In short, the real danger to the secular political arena is not vigorous religious speech, but religious speech that is effectively unopposed because potential opponents gag themselves with a broken taboo.

Fortunately, it turns out that voices are emerging that take up, redirect, and recode socially and politically conservative Christian dialects. They are coming not from the secular left or liberalism, but from within the larger religious community.

One must know well the language and practices of one's political and cultural others in order to revoice them, so the questions to ask are: Who knows best the language and practices of fundamentalism and the religious right? Who is in the best position to revoice them in contexts that pluralize points of view within those discourses? The obvious answer is, other Christians, some of them liberal, lapsed, or ethnic Christians, but most of them theologically conservative evangelical Christians who, one way or another, beg to differ with the religious right.[8]

A loose, tacit, and growing coalition of voices, left, right, and center, has turned "social justice" into a mainstream white evangelical issue, even putting it on a par theologically with "personal salvation." The evangelical left (Jim Wallis, Ron Sider, Tony Campolo) rose from the undead, and politically ambiguous evangelical figures (Rick Warren, Richard Cizik, Gregory Boyd, Brian McLaren, even the Irish rock star Bono) are coming into focus, sometimes with surprising force. There are news stories about antiwar protests at evangelical colleges, gay evangelical Bible study groups, green evangelical initiatives, and alliances between evangelicals and ACT UP.

What we are seeing is that the category "evangelical," in spite of its recent identification with the religious right, was always more diverse.[9] Many evangelicals never identified with the religious right, and an increasing number have become disillusioned with it. But more is going on than preexisting and growing political diversity. As in the period in which the religious right emerged, revoicing worldly practices feeds cultural innovation within evangelicalism. Now, however, more socially moderate evangelicals are taking the lead, and the primary targets of their revoicing practices are as much the idioms of the religious right as of liberalism.

For example, the Evangelical Environmental Network (EEN), established in 1993 but rooted in discussions among evangelicals that go back to the 1970s, is "a biblically orthodox Christian environmental organization" that construes and revoices environmentalist discourses *and* the inerrant Bible on behalf of "creation-care."[10] Nearly 500 evangelical leaders signed its Evangelical Declaration on Creation-Care in 1994.[11] In 2002, an Evangelical Environmental Network public advertising campaign in national newspapers, magazines, and television asked, "What Would Jesus Drive?"

What Would Jesus Drive?

To some, the question might seem amusing. But we take it seriously. As our Savior and Lord Jesus Christ teaches us, "Love your neighbor as yourself." *(Mk 12:30-31)*

Of all the choices we make as consumers, the cars we drive have the single biggest impact on all of God's creation.

Car pollution causes illness and death, and most afflicts the elderly, poor, sick and young. It also contributes to global warming, putting millions at risk from drought, flood, hunger and homelessness.

Transportation is now a moral choice and an issue for Christian reflection. It's about more than engineering—it's about ethics. About obedience. About loving our neighbor.

So what *would* Jesus drive?

We call upon America's automobile industry to manufacture more fuel-efficient vehicles. And we call upon Christians to drive them.

Because it's about more than vehicles—it's about values.

Rev. Clive Calver, Ph.D.
President, World Relief

Rev. Richard Cizik
Vice President for Governmental Affairs, National Association of Evangelicals

Loren Cunningham
Founder, Youth with a Mission
President, University of the Nations

Rev. David H. Englehard, Ph.D.
General Secretary, Christian Reformed Church in North America

Millard Fuller
Founder & President, Habitat for Humanity International

Rev. Vernon Grounds, Ph.D.
Chancellor, Denver Seminary

Rev. Steve Hayner, Ph.D.
Past President, InterVarsity Christian Fellowship

Rev. Roberta Hestenes, Ph.D.
International Minister, World Vision

Rev. Richard Mouw, Ph.D.
President, Fuller Theological Seminary

Rev. Ron Sider, Ph.D.
President, Evangelicals for Social Action

Sponsored By THE EVANGELICAL ENVIRONMENTAL NETWORK
10 East Lancaster Ave., Wynnewood, PA 19096 www.WhatWouldJesusDrive.org
Partial list of signatories. Affiliations listed for identification only.

What Would Jesus Drive? God saw that it was good, and Jesus says, love they neighbor as thyself. Yet too many of the cars, trucks, and SUVs that are made, that we choose to drive are polluting the air, increasing global warming, changing the weather, and endangering our health, especially the health of our children. So if we love our neighbor and we cherish God's creation, maybe we should ask, what would Jesus drive?[12]

The campaign, full of eye- and ear-catching ironies, deftly redirected and reinscribed biblical orthodoxy about creation as it appropriated and resignified a classic nineteenth-century image of Jesus as well as the morally conservative teen-oriented inflection of "What would Jesus do?" (abstinence from sex, and so forth), which was itself a recoding of the question coined in the 1920s, when it carried connotations of good works and abstinence from drinking.[13]

More recently, the National Association of Evangelicals (NAE), under the leadership of its vice president, Richard Cizik, has taken up the cause of creation-care and in 2005 enlisted eighty-six mainstream evangelical leaders to sign a statement on global climate change.[14] These and a number of other initiatives and organizations distinguish themselves explicitly and, by their use of Bible-based language, implicitly from (their caricature of) liberals and environmentalism,[15] at the same time as they forcefully argue essentially the same case for global warming. The simultaneous appropriation and distancing from—the revoicing of—religious right single-issue politics by some green evangelicals is at times blatant: Cizik and EEN co-founder Jim Ball attended the 2005 March for Life in Washington, D.C., carrying a banner that read, "Stop Mercury Poisoning of the Unborn."

Religious right leaders have responded to this challenge from their evangelical kin, attacking in particular Richard Cizik and the Evangelical Climate Initiative. James Dobson, head of Focus on the Family, accused Climate Initiative spokesman Cizik of "dividing evangelicals," urged his radio listeners not to let environmental "doomsday theories" distract them from abortion and same-sex marriage, and joined other religious right leaders in calling for Cizik's ouster from the NAE.[16]

Former vice president Al Gore's mainstream film, *An Inconvenient Truth*, may be seen as an instance of secular environmental apocalypticism, but some reviewers and viewers caught its distinctly evangelical form and tone.[17] Specifically, in *An Inconvenient Truth*, Al Gore, a lifelong practicing Baptist who attended divinity school, preached an "American jeremiad," a Protestant political sermon that laments "that a people has fallen into sinful ways and face ruin unless they swiftly reform."[18] Doom is imminent but conditional, not inevitable. It can be reversed by human action, but time is short.

A jeremiad, invariably, is a message people do not want to hear, so the life of the preacher-prophet is a hard one. "I've been trying to tell this story for a long time," Al Gore says, "and I feel as if I've failed to get the message across." Over the years, he has taken his message to many high places, and he has suffered trials and tribulations. "So-called skeptics," among them presidents and his fellow senators, ignore and scoff him. When his son was at death's door, he asked himself, "How should I spend this time on earth?" When his sister died from lung cancer after a life of smoking cigarettes, he realized "that there can be a day [a day of reckoning] when you wish you had connected the dots more quickly." Losing the presidential election, he recalled, "was a hard blow. It brought into focus the mission I had been pursuing all these years." He has seen others carrying the message suffer as well: "I've seen scientists who were persecuted, ridiculed, deprived of jobs, income, simply because the facts they'd discovered led them to an unconventional truth . . . that they insisted on telling." He believes we can turn things around. Redemption is possible. Our world, the planet earth, the future of civilization is at stake: "I believe this is a moral issue. It is

your time to seize this issue. It is our time to rise again and secure our future."[19]

Is this just another unfortunate incursion of religious rhetoric
into the secular arena? I don't think so. According to the literary
scholar Sacvan Bercovitch, the jeremiad has played a significant
role throughout the development of modern American political
culture. "Its function was to create a climate of anxiety that
helped release the restless 'progressivist' energies" that motivate
collective social and political projects.[20] The jeremiad continues
to do such work, but lately it has done so mostly on behalf of
right-wing and fundamentalist Christian projects. Al Gore's is
the first efficacious opposition to those religious-right jeremiads,
the first to oppose them not merely through nay-saying and critique, but through performance, performance that takes up the
voice, the narrative, and the rhetorical forms currently dominated by the religious right and swerves them to other ends.

Al Gore's movie performs a powerful alternative conditional
apocalyptic as compared to the ones articulated by the *Left Behind* series, dominion theology, and end-timers such as the
Christian Four Wheelers who read Micah 4:2—"Come let us
go up on the mountains"—as an invitation to tear up the moun-
tainsides with all-terrain vehicles because "global environmental
annihilation is a divine requirement for Christ's return."[21] And
it works as an alternative precisely because of its aggressively religious and specifically Christian Protestant undertows.[22]

LOOKING BACK over the broad sweep of American political
history, it is difficult to understand how so many of us became
convinced that "religion and politics don't mix" in our public
life. Not that there should be no separation of church and state.

Nor that there are not serious ways that separation has been breached under the influence of the religious right. But the notion that we could ever rid public discourse of religious idioms, tropes, and narratives, or that churches would cease to have a significant role in shaping and organizing us as political subjects now seems quite far-fetched. Nor is there any way to exclude "extreme" religious voices as opposed to "moderate" ones.

The only way to check extreme religious voices is to oppose them, and that opposition must include insider revoicings that are immersed in the rhetorical forms and perform them with a difference. Reason, explanation, critique, counterargument, alternative "framings," resistance, oppositional politics, parody, blasphemy, vilification, and attack are not enough. The political, cultural, and linguistic territory of movements such as the religious right must be occupied, colonized, and re-landscaped from the perspective of other internal, but alien, points of view. If insider revoicings of the religious right gain density, diversity, and charisma, the result will not be the end of secularity, any more than it would be the reinstallation of a narrow secularity that relies on everyone playing by the rules of a-religious reason. It would be instead a more "robust secularity"[23] in which access to all kinds of rhetorical and narrative resources, including religious ones, is widely distributed.

What would Orwell say? His foes were bad writing, doublethink, thought police, and Totalitarianism of any political stripe. He also joined the century-long European rebellion against religion insofar as it was "a lie, a semi-conscious device for keeping the rich rich and the poor poor" through the promise of a better life in the world beyond the grave.[24] But Orwell's literary revoicings of the horrors of twentieth-century Totalitarianism in *Animal Farm* and *1984* were not directed at religion.

Writing in 1940, he suggested that, if anything, the revolt against religion, through its "amputation of the soul," had helped create "the nightmare we are now enduring." "Human types supposedly extinct for centuries, the dancing dervish, the robber chieftain, the Grand Inquisitor, have suddenly reappeared, not as inmates of lunatic asylums, but as the masters of the world."[25] For him, "the soul" was "the belief in human brotherhood," and the key passage from Karl Marx was not "religion is the opium of the people" but "religion is the sigh of the soul in a soulless world."[26] Were Orwell to look back at the long wake of the Falwellians now that others seem to be taking steerage of white public Protestantism in America, he might at least wonder if some soul will resurface amid the turbulence and human debris.

PART THREE

Media and Message

Welcome to
the Infotainment Freak Show

Martin Kaplan

In the year 1984, reflecting on the book *1984*, sociologist Neil Postman gave a series of lectures at the University of Southern California Annenberg School for Communication in which he raised the question: Were Americans doomed to inhabit George Orwell's authoritarian dystopia? His answer: No. We were veering instead toward the hedonic world depicted in Aldous Huxley's *Brave New World* and were in imminent danger of amusing ourselves to death.

The pathology Postman diagnosed derived from what he termed the epistemology of entertainment, which was on the verge of displacing the epistemology of the Enlightenment. Entertainment substitutes juxtaposition for order, storytelling for truth telling, graphics for texts, sensation for reason, spectacle for seriousness, combat for discourse, play for purpose, sizzle for steak. "Our priests and presidents," he wrote, "our surgeons and lawyers, our educators and newscasters need worry less about satisfying the demands of their discipline than the demands of good showmanship. Had Irving Berlin changed one word in the title of his celebrated song, he would have been as prophetic, albeit more terse, as Aldous Huxley. He need only have written, There's No Business But Show Business."[1]

Today, the clock strikes thirteen every hour in America. That startling digit is not evidence that Big Brother rules, but rather that entertainment reigns. In contemporary America, and arguably in most industrial democracies, the imperative of practically every domain of human existence is to grab and hold the attention of audiences. In politics, it is now more important for a candidate to have big name recognition, and the money to buy big media, than it is to have big ideas. In news, it is absolutely essential to have high ratings, but it is only optional to have high accuracy. These days, a university can get by with average scholarship, but without a strong brand identity in the educational marketplace, it will surely perish. A museum that fails to mount blockbuster traveling shows, complete with a killer gift shop, is on a fast track to losing revenues, patrons, and public subsidies. To attract tourists, cities now turn to starchitects, whose glitzy creations rival Hollywood and Babel. Commerce, once about goods and services, is today about experiences and aspirations; every store promises a little bit of Disneyland. Even our interior lives are played out through the tropes of entertainment. It is now normal to experience clothing as wardrobe, furniture as set decoration, other people as characters, conversation as dialogue, and events as plot points in the narratives of our life stories, which come complete with voice-overs and flashbacks.

Postman's jeremiad clearly failed to stem entertainment's tide, just as Orwell's fables failed to vanquish Totalitarianism. Our present moment in the history of consciousness is widely known as postmodernity—"pomo," in a fun shorthand fitting for the age of show business. In the first part of the twentieth century,

Karl Popper said that philosophy's task was to demarcate between what is scientific and what is not, and he linked the project of science to the robustness of open societies. But by the twilight of that century, pomo intellectuals were declaring the Popperian project dead, and their doppelgängers in popular culture have since been dancing on its grave. By now we all know the postmodern mantra: Objective knowledge is a mirage. There is no such thing as epistemology without a knowing subject. Science is no longer a privileged realm, designed to weigh the truth of competing claims, but is yet another act in the pomo circus, where knowledge based on rigorous trial and error is on the same footing as all other tribal belief systems. All reality is socially constructed. Everything, even truth, is politics. Politics, once conceived as the craft of decisionmaking, has been remade as the art of attention getting. Communication, rather than striving to convey truth and meaning, now prizes informing an audience less than *having* an audience. The public interest has been redefined as what the public is interested in; the public sphere has become a theater, where citizenship is a performance.

Orwell famously worried about the divorce of public discourse, including journalism, from truth, but he did not anticipate its remarriage to entertainment. Journalism, whose practitioners in high-end newspapers and early broadcast outlets once saw their task as recording the truth, now largely functions to hold up a mirror for us to see our fun-house reflection. The old journalistic paradigm posited a search for accuracy, objectivity, and fairness. The new pomo paradigm declares those goals misbegotten; they are inherently unachievable. Because everyone possesses and advocates for his or her own truth, the job of the reporter is not to adjudicate among competing assertions, but to assemble them into a de facto collage. The fairness of contemporary journalism resembles not the fairness of a judge and jury weighing evidence within a framework of rules, but rather the fairground of the carnival midway, where barkers call out on behalf of their wares.

Whereas accuracy can never be achieved, "balance"—the new lowest common denominator and deceptive battle cry—is an easy goal; all you need to do is open up your airwaves and column inches to everyone. Better yet, open the public square to combatants, in polarized pairs. There's no surer way to attract an audience than a bear fight, and no dispute is too nuanced not to be reducible by modern journalism to he-says versus she-says. Instead of trying to tell us what's true, journalism now prides itself on finding two sides to every story, no matter how feeble one side may be. There's no grand narrative making sense of the progression of current events; there are just dueling narratives, competing story lines, alternate and equally plausible ways to connect the dots. It's as though a generation of journalists has been weaned on Jacques Derrida and deconstruction, and their only recourse in the Dada zoo is pastiche.

In such a carnivalesque media ecology, people are patsies for propagandists. Even if a near majority of authorities holds one view about reality (on the causes of global warming, say, or the validity of evolution, the risks of mercury pollution, the existence of WMD in Iraq, the success of abstinence-only as a sex education strategy), a television "news" booker is always delighted to invite a fringe spokesperson onto a program as "balance," to convey the notion that these are all wide-open questions. Journalists have recused themselves from ranking the legitimacy of "experts," so corporate and political front groups with lofty names (Discovery Institute, Heritage Foundation, National Center for Policy Analysis, National Association of Scholars, et al.) have the same opportunity to inject themselves into public debate as research institutions that still cling to old-fashioned standards of evidence and accuracy. These "think tanks" *manufacture* debate. That's what they do: Their aim is to create the illusion of controversy, even when the facts are indisputable, because they know how enslaved contemporary journalism is by the tyranny of false equivalence. What's more, the louder you are, the more outrageous your claim, the less civil your discourse, the farther you stand from common ground, the more welcome you will be as a guest and a source. It is not necessary to be right; to make the sale, it is only necessary to get attention.

The old paradigm depended on a hierarchy of gatekeepers. Within journalistic institutions, reporters were vetted by editors, copy editors, and executives; judgments were tempered by the time span of the daily news cycle. Among journalistic outlets, print publications set the gold standard, and national newspapers set the standard among them. But now, the brand names of old-guard institutions mean little to mass audiences. The Internet has made everyone a reporter, videographer, and distributor of content. This may well be a good thing in itself, but the Internet is also putting out to pasture the professionals who presided over the accumulation, fairness, and accuracy of the news.

The need to hold audiences round the clock has put a premium not on the information journalists see as important for citizens to know, but instead on the "content" that corporate owners bet will mesmerize consumers. The turning point probably came in the mid-1980s, when CBS News discovered that *60 Minutes* could be a reliable cash cow. Today, nearly universally, news is programmed not as a public service but as a profit center. Its messages are designed to appeal to humans' hardwiring. In Johan Huizinga's formulation, we are not *Homo sapiens*, the creature who knows; we are *Homo ludens*, the creature who plays. Like it or not, our species is a sucker for novelty, sex, fear, pictures, motion, noise, scatology, fun; we can't stop our eyes from turning toward celebrity and spectacle. Journalism's job today is not to find and deliver us the worthwhile hidden in the muck, but rather to stream the muck at us, 24/7, and to sell our captive eyeballs to advertisers.

When Ted Turner launched CNN in 1980, there were high hopes for the broad diffusion of news. The results of the twenty-five-year experiment in round-the-clock cable "news," which now includes Fox and MSNBC, are now in. Here's what cable news is really good at: trapped miners, Michael Jackson, runaway brides, missing blondes, Christmas Eve murders, Princess Di, Paris Hilton, hurricanes, tsunamis, disinformation, whiz-bang graphics, scary theme music, polls, gotcha, HeadOn ads, "Thanks for having me," people who begin every answer to antagonistic questions with "Look," people who say, "I didn't interrupt you when *you* were talking," and anchors who say, "We'll have to leave it there." Here's what cable news is not so good at: insight, context, depth, reflection, proportion, perspective, relevance, humility, information, analysis, *news*.

There is nothing that pomo news likes more than Armageddon. When the Hezbollah kidnapping of Israeli soldiers in 2006 escalated into a war between Israel and Lebanon, it was covered as a tinderbox about to explode, a downward-spiraling crisis, the tipping point of a regional conflagration, the start of World War III. We were told it could trigger an oil crisis worse than the one in the late 1970s, resulting in gas lines and rationing and $20-per-gallon at the pump. It could spark worldwide inflation, recession, depression. It was the most dangerous moment since (fill in the blank). To be sure, it was a dangerous situation. But much of what the news media delivered was in fact crisis porn, fed to an insatiable audience, and itself a likely cause of the escalation of the crisis.

Journalism, especially television journalism, has tremendous ability to control the tone of what it covers. The quantity, the music, the graphics, the word choices can all be dialed up or down. The notion that professional news judgment—a reliable journalistic rule book—is what really drives the nature and kind of coverage is hopelessly quaint. The truth is that a missing white woman can easily be turned by the media machine into a global red-alert, and a holocaust in Africa can be marginalized as a sidebar story. When it comes to holding audiences' attention, the only thing better than suspense is suspense about carnage, and the only thing better than suspense about carnage is suspense about the apocalypse. Terrorists, especially stateless terrorists, depend on the media's addiction to fear and crisis. They have gamed the media system; they bank on getting their message amplified. This is not to diminish the legitimate news value of the horrors they perpetrate. But it's also true that attempts to cool things off, reduce tensions, and back off from the brink are at odds with the sexy Nielsens that accompany real-time coverage of the end of the world. It is chilling that the arbiter we used to rely on for the facts is itself now a stakeholder with a vested interest in imagining the worst.

The firing, in the spring of 2007, of radio host Don Imus was depicted as a victory for civil discourse. In reality, the most important thing to know about Don Imus is that he was a financial gusher for Viacom and General Electric until his advertisers began peeling away. The only reason that shock jocks are on the air in the first place is that people pay attention to them. We lend our ears to Imus and his ilk because outrageousness amuses us. A merely curmudgeonly cowboy would not have pulled big numbers, and neither the political class nor the punditocracy would have returned his bookers' calls. What made the powerful kiss Imus's ring, and what made people tune in, was how bad-boy—how rude, disrespectful, licking-the-razor—he was. Clearly, large audiences liked to gasp at what he got away with, and CBS and NBC were champs at spinning those oh-my-Gods into ka-chings.

The same could still be said of the envelope-pushing by Rush Limbaugh, Ann Coulter, Glenn Beck, Sean Hannity, Michael Savage, and the dozens of other acts in the infotainment freak show. Their *effect* may be to debase discourse, inflame prejudice, sow ignorance, exculpate criminality, incite rancor, ruin reputations, and stoke the right-wing base—but their effect is not their job. Their *job* is to make money—for the media conglomerates that employ them. We may revile them for being demagogues, but we are chumps if we ignore how relentlessly the companies that employ them monetize their noxious shtick. Those corporations are not in the news business, nor the public interest business, nor the patriotism business. They're in the profit business.

Imagine if the audience's appetite for outrage extended to the atrophy of American democracy. Imagine if media bosses believed that we were insatiable for information about the apparent attempt to rig the 2008 election by politicizing the Justice Department and prosecuting phony voter fraud. Imagine if the same kind of blanket coverage that's currently conferred

on loopy astronauts, bratty rehaboholics, and slandered bas-
ketball teams were afforded instead to the assault on civil liberties and democratic processes now underway in America.
Would we watch it the same Pavlovian way we watch tits,
twits, and tornadoes?

Media executives think not. They don't believe the jury is still
out on that one. They don't think that we're addicted to junk
news and shock jocks because it's the only diet they've offered
us; they think the market for civically useful information is simply saturated. And they don't think that way because they're just
tools of the vast right-wing conspiracy (though some, like Fox,
have made that their market niche) or because it serves their
economic self-interest (though the tax cuts and wealth transfers
whose consequences they've declined to cover have benefited
them handsomely). No, they air what they air, and cover what
they cover, as a capitalist service *to us*. Us, in the form of our
mutual funds, our pension funds, our IRAs and 401(k)s, our
collective American existence as Wall Street. Entertainment is
exquisitely sensitive to demand. As long as we demand quarterly growth in profits more aggressively than we demand real
news, the clowns will always get more airtime than the fifth
column of hacks who have penetrated the halls of Justice.

Surely this knack for pandering to our taste for sensational-
ism is not why the news business is the only for-profit enterprise to be protected by the Constitution. Nor is it likely that
the modern journalistic project, defined as the imperative to obtain market share, will do its part to deliver the educated citizenry that Thomas Jefferson said democracy depends on.
Perhaps the Internet, by exponentially increasing the number of
channels through which we can receive news, and by enabling

new knowledge-networks that can be mobilized for information gathering, will prove to be a powerful antidote to the brave new world of entertainment *über alles*. But it is just as possible that the need to monetize cyberspace will have the same consequences for online information that it has had in the old media. On the Internet, no one knows if you're Big Brother.

Neither Snow, Nor Rain, Nor Heat, Nor Gloom of Night Will Stay the Couriers from the Swift Completion of Their Appointed Rounds— but What About Big Media?

Victor Navasky

George Orwell alerted us to two great dangers: first, what he feared and fought and wrote against—the totalitarian state, the closed society, censorship, book banning, that is, everything represented by Big Brother; and second, the abuse and misuse of his beloved English language. Not just the doublespeak of *1984*, but also, as he writes in "Politics and the English Language," the possibility that the corruption of the English language could corrupt clear thinking.

I would suggest that by the late twentieth century, a third danger had arrived on the scene, which anyone who purports to care about democracy and the public sphere (as did Orwell) would do well to ponder.

Marshall McLuhan famously instructed us that the medium is the message. Fair enough, but some media are more equal than others. These days, especially in the United States, concentrated media, or what I refer to as Big Media, may have replaced Big Brother as the principal danger to the open public dialogue that makes democracy possible.

Big Media is not a fear but a fact. In 1983, the media critic Ben Bagdikian wrote *The Media Monopoly,* a book that definitively documented the future of media concentration. By the 1980s, the majority of all major American media—newspapers, magazines, radio, television, books, and movies—was controlled by fifty giant corporations.

These corporations were "interlocked in common financial interest with other massive corporate entities and with a few dominant international banks." They espoused a shared ideology. Bagdikian accused them of self-serving censorship and of perpetuating a series of myths to prop up the status quo (government spending was "out of control," corporate taxes were "crushing," the graduated income tax "unfairly strikes the wealthy," and so on). One can argue about whether Bagdikian was right, but his more important message was incontrovertible: Concentration leads to homogenization.

In a deliberate Orwellian echo, Bagdikian noted, "The fifty men and women who dominate these corporations would fit in a large room. They constitute a new Ministry of Information and Culture." Bagdikian presciently predicted that by the end of the century, the number would be down to a mere half a dozen.

THE ACTIVIST-SCHOLAR Robert McChesney and the journalist John Nichols, among others, have written extensively about the ways in which Big Media has undermined free expression, discouraged creativity, marginalized radical ideas, distorted the public dialogue, and generally disserved democracy. Veteran television journalist Bill Moyers observed, "Big media is ravenous. It never gets enough, always wants more. And it will stop at nothing to get it. These conglomerates are an empire. And they are imperial."

Michael J. Copps, commissioner of the Federal Communications Commission, took the trouble to write an op-ed piece in the *New York Times,* arguing that "[u]nder pressure from media conglomerates previous commissions have eviscerated the [broadcast license] renewal process. Now we get what big broadcasters lovingly call 'postcard renewal'—the agency typically rubber-stamps an application without any substantive review." And though an argument can be made that the growth of the Internet and modern telecommunications, combined with the new media's unique capacity for interactivity, enhances the potential for a truly democratic media system, Jeff Chester (whom Moyers has dubbed "the Paul Revere of the media revolution") makes a convincing case in his book *Digital Destiny* that the country's most powerful communications companies are using their financial and political heft to solidify control over the new media as well. Rather than bringing forth the "global information commons" that digital visionaries have been dreaming about, the Internet, too, may yet succumb to Big Media.

Speaking as a magazine person (I write, edit, publish, and teach them), let me cite by way of example the impact of one of Bagdikian's communications behemoths on two old media institutions that were very much around in Orwell's day, are still with us, and are in my opinion more critical than ever to the open society that Orwell cared so much about: One is the journal of opinion (which the philosopher Jürgen Habermas in effect has identified as house organ to the public sphere); the other—not generally thought of as a communications medium, but perhaps our most important one—is the postal system. Good old snail mail. What good, after all, would a magazine of opinion be if it couldn't end up in the mailbox of a thoughtful citizen?

The journal of opinion was one of Orwell's favorite platforms. He wrote frequently for magazines like the *New Statesman* (whose reluctance to print his dispatches from civil-war Spain undoubtedly informed the anti-totalitarian theme of *Animal Farm*), produced a weekly column ("As I Please") for London's left-wing *Tribune*), and contributed a regular "Letter from London" to *Partisan Review*.

In *Arguing the World*, Joseph Dorman's documentary on New York intellectuals in the years following World War II, the filmmaker quotes the novelist Saul Bellow's observation, "When you published something in *Partisan Review* it was likely to be flanked by Ignazio Silone on one side and George Orwell on the other, and you had finally found a place for yourself among the leading figures of the century. And that was very exciting. There was an internationalization of the intellectuals in those years."

Of course not every journal of opinion has the clout that *Partisan Review* had in its heyday. But some opinion-making journals—take the example of the *New York Review of Books* today—play a role similar to that of *Partisan Review* in earlier times. The *New York Review*'s circulation is more than ten times that of the *Partisan Review*. It is as true in the early years of the twenty-first century as it was in the middle years of the twentieth that journals of this sort have a cultural and political impact disproportionate to their circulation. Although opinion magazines aren't quite as trendy as the blogosphere, these artifacts from the Age of Print, if that is what they are, almost by definition speak with an authority and command an influence that is unmatched by ephemeral sound bites or 750-word messages that are here today and disappear into cyberspace tomorrow.

But it was no accident (to use a turn of phrase favored by *Partisan* contributors) that in early 2007, when the U.S. Postal Service announced a rate change that worked to the particular disadvantage of small political journals of opinion that it was implemented at the behest of one of Bagdikian's communications behemoths, of which more follows below.

The new postal policy hit smaller periodicals (and particularly journals of opinion, which characteristically carry little advertising and for the most part already operate at a loss) with a much larger postal rate rise than that levied on the largest, most opulent magazines. Countless little mags could be forced out of business, and it will become difficult if not impossible for smaller companies to launch new journals. The *Nation,* which is in better shape than most small circulation magazines, has estimated that the new mail charges will cost it a minimum of a half million dollars in the first year.

How did this ill-advised and unprecedented action come to pass?

A little history is in order: The founding fathers of this country believed that the circulation of information, opinion, and what they called intelligence was a necessary condition to self-governance. They saw the postal service as the circulatory system of democracy. The mail, as Richard R. John[1] put it, facilitated "an imagined community that incorporated a far-flung citizenry into the political process." The postal system helped transform the country from a confederation of separate states into "one great neighborhood."

That, among other reasons, is why Benjamin Franklin agreed to serve as postmaster general. That is why Thomas Jefferson sought to persuade George Washington to name Thomas Paine as postmaster general. That is also why Washington himself believed that all newspapers (the equivalent of today's journals of opinion) should be delivered free of charge. In defense of the view that newspapers should be mailed free, Representative Eldridge Gerry of Massachusetts, a delegate to the Constitutional Convention, declared in 1791 that "wherever information is freely circulated, there slavery doesn't exist; or if it does, it will vanish as soon as information has been generally diffused."

This is not the place to provide a comprehensive history of the post office, but students of its contribution to American democracy would do well to keep four dates in mind:

- The Post Office Act of 1792, which charged newspapers admitted into the mails a token fee, but well below the costs of conveyance.

- The Post Office Act of 1879 which created the category of second-class mail, put newspapers and magazines on the same footing, and signaled the emergence of the mass circulation magazine.

- The Postal Reorganization Act of 1970, which established the U.S. Postal Service, a semi-independent corporation whose mission was "to bind the country together." But the Nixon-appointed Board of Governors of the new USPS interpreted the act (over the objections of the historian Arthur Schlesinger Jr.) as a decree that each class of mail must pay its own way, a dramatic departure from the idea of the founders. The deadline for the implementation of this radical repeal of almost 200 years of postal policy was, appropriately enough, 1984!

- The postal rate increase of 2007, when for the first time the postal service, which had until that time imposed rate increases on big and small periodicals more or less equally, adopted a plan and rate structure that Time Warner's lawyer-lobbyists had been pushing for more than a decade, all in the name of efficiency.

The full behind-the-scenes story of how the 2007 rate increase came to pass has yet to be told, but it was perhaps inevitable that the world's largest magazine company (Time Warner publishes more than 100 periodicals) would persuade the USPS, which is itself a monopoly (and long the country's largest employer), that in the name of "efficiency" it ought to adopt an Orwellian plan whereby the smaller the magazine, the higher the postal rates. Needless to say, this newsworthy reversal of a public policy dating back to the beginning of the republic received little or no coverage in the conglomerated, mainstream media.

What is to be done?

First, we must take advantage of what George Orwell did know about—politics and the English language—and not permit what little debate there has been about this critical aspect of the public sphere to be carried on in what I can only call postal-speak.

When Time Warner testifies before the Postal Regulatory Commission its argument has been that by mailing in bulk from different entry points around the country, they save the postal service money and therefore they should be charged less. Over the years, their lawyer-lobbyists make their case by pointing out the company's contributions in terms of "pre-sorting" and "drop shipping" by zip code, "palletizing" (in bundles of twenty-four or more), "co-mailing," and "zoning." Putting aside the fact that small circulation magazines lack the resources to "drop ship" (which often means printing simultaneously at various plants around the country and long-distance trucking), they can't "pre-sort" by zip code in bundles of twenty-four or more because in many zip codes they only have one or two subscribers, and the new "zoning" surcharges appear designed to force mailers to bypass the USPS, in effect privatizing this historic service. (It used to be that surcharges were only imposed on advertising content—editorial content always traveled at one rate, no matter how great the distance.)

In any event, the issue obviously isn't only efficiency. The postal authorities should keep the democratic mission of the postal service in mind and should take into consideration how to balance the dubious requirement that each class of mail break even. How do we achieve cost savings and simultaneously give space to minority and dissenting voices? Providing a solution to that puzzle is what democracy in general and these journals in particular—left, right, libertarian, and communitarian—are all about.

The problem of Big Media's impact on the political culture does not stop with the postal frustrations of small political magazines. I have not even pretended to deal here with books, television, movies, and the new media. Information, ideas, intelligence, and opinions are not commodities. They should not be left to the vicissitudes of the market or the distortions of Big Media. As Bagdikian predicted, by the end of the last century the number of culture-dominating Big Media companies was down to the single digits. Today, with another wave of buyouts and mergers sweeping the economy, the trend continues. Whatever happened to antitrust? As far as the new media are concerned, it is all very well to talk about the interactive potential of the Internet for globalized democracy. But if Stanford University law professor Lawrence Lessig is right, "Powerful conglomerates are swiftly using both law and technology to 'tame' the Internet" so that it "will be directed from the top down, increasingly controlled by owners of the networks, holders of the largest patent portfolios, and most invidiously, hoarders of copyrights."

We are talking about the public sphere here, not mustard or shaving cream. Diversity of choice in this regard is not a convenience or a luxury but an essential ingredient of a healthy democracy. We should not leave such matters either to Big Media or small-minded bureaucrats who look the other way when issues of social policy come along. If the newly raised postal rates mean that in the future it will be increasingly difficult for small companies to publish independent magazines, then it's important to recognize that these are not merely bureaucratic but also political issues.

An informed and empowered citizenry is necessary for a diversity of viewpoints to become part of the political debate. One way to ensure the diversity of our media would be to demand (ask) that our candidates for public office put forward an information policy the same way they put forward a foreign or a domestic policy.

As they commission their papers on media and democracy, the candidates might want to consult Free Press, the public interest group founded by Robert McChesney, which organizes conferences and runs campaigns and calls itself "a national, non-partisan media reform organization." They ought to read and listen to Jeff Chester, who still believes that if properly regulated, the growth of the Internet and interactive telecommunications can accelerate the emergence of a truly democratic media system. And let's remember the injunction of the late Jim Carey, the Columbia University journalism professor, who once proposed that we think of journalism as "an exercise in poetry." The challenge is to persuade the public to come back to politics as active participants and cease to sit passively before a discussion conducted by experts and transcribed by journalists. Journalists, along with everybody else in the communications business, should carry on the national (and international) conversation that will occupy, shape, and ultimately define the public sphere.

IN THE SUMMER OF 1948, George Orwell wrote, "If we find ourselves in ten years' time cringing before somebody like [the Soviet Communist leader Andrei] Zhdanov, it will probably be because that is what we have deserved." His point was not that there were strong tendencies toward Totalitarianism at work within the English literary intelligentsia, although there may have been. His point was that this was a political age and it was the obligation of the writer, the intellectual, and the informed citizen to resist the dominant orthodoxy. Today, I would suggest that Big Media functions to inculcate, disseminate, and propagate (often by mere assumption) the dominant orthodoxy. Historically, the best journals of opinion have functioned as voices of dissent, putting new issues on the public agenda, questioning the dominant orthodoxy. In the current case, primarily through everybody else's inattention, Big Media has manipulated the old postal medium to advance its own fortunes at the expense of its mini-brethren.

In previous times, these small-circulation political and cultural journals have provided the space for reasoned argument in their fields of interest. There are those who would argue that in ten years' time, the Internet and the blogosphere will render these journals obsolete.

I don't think so. I don't think that the high-speed, un-fact-checked blogosphere, where articles longer than 1,000 words are discouraged, will ever replace the journal of opinion, which provides the space and context to set the standard for reasoned discourse. In my mind, the blog is to the journal of opinion as the paperback is to the hardcover—it will, if anything, extend the audience for serious political and cultural commentary rather than replace it. But if we permit the blogosphere, along with the rest of the media, to continue either to be absorbed by or to take over Big Media, the dominant orthodoxy will carry the day and we will have only ourselves to blame.

Reporters and Rhetoric

GEOFFREY COWAN

Nothing has the capacity to frame political debate more successfully than a good turn of phrase, characterization, or metaphor; nor can anything do more to pervert democratic discourse than inaccurate, imprecise, or misleading language. George Orwell understood the game and called its bluff more than sixty years ago. In words that offered an eerie forecast of the rhetoric of Vietnam, he noted that "[d]efenceless villages are bombarded from the air, the inhabitants driven out into the countryside, the cattle machine-gunned, the huts set on fire with incendiary bullets: this is called *pacification*."

He understood, too, that political advocates trade in the use of language. Since "there is no agreed definition" of the word *democracy*, Orwell noted, "the defenders of every kind of régime claim that it is a democracy. . . ." This is one area where the world has not really changed since 1946, when Orwell wrote "Politics and the English Language." Nor, indeed since a quarter of a century before that, when Walter Lippmann in *Public Opinion* described the role of "the publicity man" who shapes images for reporters, acting as "censor and propagandist, responsible only to his employers," presenting the truth "only as it accords with the employer's conception of his own interest."

But while political advocates and press agents have always had every right (and every incentive) to pedal their own version of the truth, and to spin their own clever phrases and metaphors, journalists should not blindly parrot their words. And once in a while, they *don't*.

In late November 2006, when NBC News first used the words *civil war* to describe events in Iraq, the network took the unusual stand of defying the government in defining the war. The phrase had been employed for years by some observers inside and outside of government. But NBC's public and publicized action moved the words to the forefront of public discourse. In doing so, NBC demonstrated one of the most important functions of the mainstream media. Usually without much internal deliberation or thought, the major press outlets effectively define the terms of America's public discourse. But the careful choice of language—of the words used to describe ourselves, our adversaries, our choices, and our debates—is a core responsibility of the press.

The decision to call events in Iraq a civil war provides an excellent case study. As early as 2004, some CIA officers had been using that phrase, as had some congressional leaders, including Senator Joseph Biden. During the next two years, much of the American public came to the same conclusion. In March 2006, a *Washington Post* poll found that a majority of Americans was afraid that the fighting between Sunni and Shiite Muslims would lead to a civil war. That summer, a number of analysts and news outlets reported that there was a debate brewing in the administration over the issue—with the CIA calling for a more honest assessment and the White House resisting.

President Bush made the administration's views clear. In March 2006, Iyad Allawi, who was Iraq's interim prime minister, used the term.

"Do you agree with Mr. Allawi that Iraq has fallen into a civil war?" a reporter asked at a news conference. The president's response was unequivocal: "I do not."

Meanwhile, various news organizations were struggling with terminology. Sectarian violence seemed too soft. Civil war seemed too definitive—and too politically sensitive. As Bill Keller, the executive editor of the *New York Times,* later explained to Brooke Gladstone on National Public Radio's *On the Media:* "One of the reasons for not using it was, you know, honestly, a concern that because the White House has contended that this is not a civil war, that using the phrase amounted to a kind of political statement." So the *Times* used qualifiers, Keller explained, quoting other sources or modifying the harshness of the term "civil war" by describing Iraq as "on the brink of civil war."

In the late fall of 2006, the *Los Angeles Times,* without fanfare, started to use the term "civil war," but those words, and their implications, did not fully become national news or enter the national consciousness until late November. Then, after a particularly bloody few days in Iraq, NBC News decided to act.

Richard Engel, an NBC reporter who has been in Iraq longer than any other American television correspondent, had long felt that the country was in a civil war. On Sunday, November 26, Alexandra Wallace, who was a vice president of NBC News, consulted Engeland anchor Brian Williams, as well as a group of military leaders and historians in an effort to determine where "sectarian violence" ends and "civil war" begins. Their view was unanimous. NBC knew that its position would be controversial. But the news division was convinced that Iraq had become a civil war.

The next morning, host Matt Lauer announced on the *Today Show* that NBC had made a formal decision to use that term. Recreating some of the elements of the discussion on the previous day, Lauer engaged in a lengthy on-air dialogue with retired general Barry McCaffrey, in which they discussed NBC's decision, the meaning of the phrase "civil war," and the arguments for and against applying that term to events on the ground in Iraq.

Predictably, the White House protested. "While the situation on the ground is very serious, neither Prime Minister Maliki nor we [the Bush White House] believe that Iraq is a civil war," a spokesman for the National Security Council told reporters on Air Force One as it was making its way across the Atlantic, taking the president to meetings in the Middle East. Some conservative media critics went further, repeating the familiar charge that the press was really against American troops. "You have violent, out-of-control chaos, not civil war," Fox's Bill O'Reilly protested. "Of course, the American media is not helping anyone by oversimplifying the situation and rooting for the USA to lose in Iraq."

But while the fight over the phrase "civil war" was largely treated as a political debate, and in some quarters as a political decision, it was, in fact, much more than that. In deciding what words to use to identify the conflict, NBC was helping to insure that its reporting was accurate. Indeed, there are times when good journalists need to be as concerned with the accuracy of their language as they are with the accuracy of their facts. Unless the mainstream press uses the correct language to describe issues of public policy, then readers, viewers, and government leaders are unlikely to understand, discuss, and analyze them honestly and meaningfully.

Speaking on *Meet the Press* six months later, on June 10, 2007, former secretary of state Colin Powell offered an unapologetic appraisal of the situation when he declared:

> I have characterized it as a civil war even though the administration does not call it that. And the reason I call it a civil war is I think that allows you to see clearly what we're facing. We're facing groups that are now fighting each other: Sunnis versus Shias, Shias versus Shias, Sunnis versus al Qaeda. And it is a civil war.

Secretary Powell went on to explain how the choice of words that we use to understand the situation in Iraq relates directly to the policies we employ when he combined two particularly controversial rhetorical phrases—"civil war" and "surge"—in the following observation:

> The current strategy to deal with it, called a surge—the military surge, our part of the surge under General Petraeus—the only thing it can do is put a heavier lid on this boiling pot of civil war stew. . . .

Whereas a number of politicians and pundits were unprepared to engage in linguistic debate early in the war, by early 2007, when President Bush announced that he was planning to launch a "surge" in Iraq, they had prepared themselves to enter the rhetorical fray. As Jim Ruttenberg reported in the *New York Times* on January 10, 2007, the day of Bush's announcement:

This week has ushered in a new political battle over the language of the war: "Surge," meet "escalation."

The Democrats introduced the latter word to portray President Bush's expected proposal for a troop increase in Iraq in a negative light.

Those making the case for the word *escalation* included Senator Ted Kennedy, who reminded listeners that "[t]he Department of Defense kept assuring us that each new escalation in Vietnam would be the last. Instead, each one led only to the next." And House Speaker Nancy Pelosi, in her first week in office, used the words *escalate* and *escalation* six times during an interview on the CBS News program *Face the Nation*.

The next day, Secretary of State Condoleezza Rice argued with Senator Chuck Hagel about the proper choice of words. "I don't see it, and the president doesn't see it, as an escalation," she told Senator Hagel (R–NE). The exchange continued:

HAGEL: Putting 22,000 new troops, more troops in, is not an escalation?

RICE: Well, I think, Senator, escalation is not just a matter of how many numbers you put in. Escalation is also a question of, are you changing the strategic goal of what you're trying to do? Are you escalating . . .

HAGEL: Would you call it a decrease, and billions of dollars more that you need for it?

RICE: I would call it, Senator, an augmentation that allows the Iraqis to deal with this very serious problem that they have in Baghdad.

Interestingly, White House Spokesman Tony Snow provided a particularly appropriate analysis. At a press briefing, when reporters pressed him about the proper terminology, he noted that the terms of the debate were being framed by "focus groups." Then he urged reporters to make their own judgment.

"This is your challenge," he said. "You guys do words for a living. Figure out—rather than trying to ask Democratic or even Republican lawmakers what the proper descriptive term is, you figure it out."

There was a case to be made on both sides. The Bush administration could claim that the concept of a "surge" had been identified and embraced by the Iraq Study Group, which was somewhat true. (The Baker-Hamilton report said: "We could, however, support a short-term redeployment or surge of American combat forces to stabilize Baghdad . . . if the U.S. commander in Iraq determines that such steps would be effective.") But looking at that same language, critics could argue that the words "short-term" and "surge" are inextricably intertwined and that what the administration was proposing was not short-term, and therefore could not be properly labeled a surge.

Faced with that linguistic debate, the press overwhelmingly decided to use the word *surge* rather than *escalation*.

But Tony Snow was right. Reporters "do words" for a living. There are times when it is as important for the press to be as accurate about the use of language as it is about the reporting of facts. As Orwell pointed out, there are those who would argue that the "struggle against the abuse of language is a sentimental archaism. . . ." But Orwell felt that it was a struggle worth waging in the aftermath of the experience of World War II; and it is at least as worthwhile today.

The power of the mainstream media may, as some have argued, be on the decline. But as NBC so recently proved, it still has the ability to help define or shape debates and to help determine what language we use. Rather than allowing any political figure or administration to define the terms of public debate, reporters and editors should examine the issue for themselves and reach an honest conclusion.

As Orwell might have noted, readers, viewers, and listeners—and our own particular form of democracy—require no less.

Lessons from the War Zone

FARNAZ FASSIHI

As a student at the Graduate School of Journalism at Columbia University, one of my favorite classes was "Critical Issues," a course that explored the ethics of journalism. Our professors, the dynamic duo of the late legendary James E. Carey and Stephen Isaacs, encouraged us, sometimes provocatively, to think critically about the process of news gathering. They taught us that good journalism is a practice that holds conscience at its core. The lofty ideals we were taught in journalism school represent the backbone of a free and independent press, one of the foundations of a democratic society. The rigorous pursuit of these ideals is what often separates American journalism from the press in other parts of the world. Outside of America, journalism is often employed to bolster a political party, a government official, or a wealthy private citizen. The American press, on the contrary, prides itself on reportage that is independent, free, objective, balanced, fearless, and truthful.

For me, an Iranian American born in the United States to Iranian parents who grew up between Iran and America, the Critical Issues class embodied my reasons for pursuing a career in newspaper journalism in the United States. Here was a chance to record an unvarnished version of truth, to inform citizens and hold elected officials accountable. I wanted to become the sort of journalist who was inherently skeptical of spin. I would not rest until the coverage I was responsible for penetrated beyond calculated news snippets supplied by so-called reliable sources. I wanted to be on the front lines of news gathering because I understood that truth was to democracy as blood is to the human body. Without it, freedom would wither and die. That, at least, was the theory.

One of my most vivid recollections of journalism school is of a Critical Issues class in which we debated the dilemmas a journalist may face while covering war. Our professors placed special emphasis on the ethical quandaries of reportage from the battlefield. We were invited to consider how a journalist should behave in a situation where soldiers from one's own country are involved in the fighting. The discussion, not surprisingly, triggered an emotionally charged debate. We were presented with a hypothetical scenario in which we were at the front lines of a war and had received critical information about an impending enemy attack. In a position to inform our military contacts about the attack and thus save soldiers' lives, we were faced with the question: What would we do? And more important, what *should* we do?

As journalists in a war zone, is it our place to intervene in the course of events? Do we have an obligation to intervene if such an action could save lives or serve the interests of our nation? Some students argued that, as journalists, we are not exempt from moral responsibility. Our professors disagreed. They reminded us that a journalist is always expected to be an objective and distant participant, an aloof observer detached from the story for the sake of maintaining an unbiased perspective. We live inside an ethical bubble that demands no loyalty to people on either side of the story—only to the facts. But are we reporters first, or citizens? Can we be both without compromising our ethics?

This was in 1998. Our class discussion predated the attacks of September 11, 2001, the War on Terror that ensued, and the American invasion of Iraq.

Over the past five years, my career as an American newspaper journalist has taken me to real battlefields in Afghanistan and Iraq. I have covered both sides of the war unilaterally, traveling independently and penetrating the interiors of these countries with a small team of local translators and a driver, and I have gone on military embeds as well. The theories hammered into my head in journalism school have constantly been put to the test. And they have sometimes been shattered.

In Iraq, despite the security hurdles that hamper the press, we find ways to obtain information. We find the right words to depict the horrors of war in spite of the military minders and government officials who try to muzzle us and feed us their perspectives. Language and security don't hobble us; something deeper does. The favored American style of journalism—distant objectivity combined with the noxious fog of war—has compromised our efforts to make the powerful impact we seek in our reportage.

We have encountered plenty of routine intimidations. In Iraq, journalists who challenge the official version of events as relayed by American military sources have been accused of having an antiwar agenda and of being unpatriotic or insensitive to matters of national security. Secretary of Defense Donald Rumsfeld suggested that journalists covering the war were exaggerating the mayhem. He accused us of reporting inaccurately, even going as far as to suggest that we were guilty of treason. He said, "The steady stream of errors all seem to be of a nature to inflame the situation and give heart to terrorists and to discourage those who hope for success in Iraq."

The U.S. military has tried to manage the flow of information by expecting reporters to practice a sort of self-censorship, particularly when it comes to exposing the heart-wrenching, ugly side of war. The truth is that war is messy and brutal. There are ambushes, violent raids, civilian casualties, and tragically interrupted lives. Young soldiers get blown up; they lose limbs or die. Ordinary citizens are shell-shocked. Even at its most triumphant, war is a ghastly experience that exposes the darkest corners of the human condition.

It follows that to write about war with rose-tinted glasses is not only a disservice to readers but a practice that flies in the face of the forces that compel correspondents to cover wars. Why else put yourself in the line of danger if not to say something true and important? All the same, reporters in Iraq who have gone against the military's request to censor themselves have lost access to their stories or found themselves kicked off embeds. In the latest tactic of damage control, the military now requires that reporters obtain a signed consent from wounded soldiers before publishing images in which they are featured. This regulation, which the military contends is an act of goodwill to protect the soldier's privacy, effectively bans powerful pictures from the battlefield that could resonate with the public back home.

In the past four years, the U.S. military has arrested reporters, mostly Iraqis, for having advance knowledge of an attack on coalition forces. According to the Committee to

Protect Journalists, these reporters worked mostly as cameramen or photographers for CBS News, Reuters, The Associated Press, and Agence France-Presse. They were detained because they showed up too quickly at the scene of an ambush or a car bomb. The military has accused the journalists, who have been detained without being charged officially with an offense, of collaborating with insurgents. In journalism school, we were told to document unflinchingly everything we saw and heard: We had a duty to the public, and to democracy. The detained Iraqi reporters who have followed this rule of thumb have been labeled criminals by U.S. authorities.

In 2003–2004, when the United States formally occupied Iraq, the military and the Coalition Provisional Authority (CPA) held daily press conferences. The briefings were useful for getting quick updates or sound bites for a story, but the general tone offered an important strategic motive: to convince us that Iraq was faring well. The military spokesperson, General Mark Kimmitt, often concluded his opening comments in an upbeat, chirpy voice declaring (I paraphrase here) that "the Coalition continues offensive operations to establish a stable Iraq in order to repair infrastructure, stimulate the economy, and transfer sovereignty."

This particular comment never failed to irk my Iraqi translator, who accompanied me to the briefings. Outside of the protected Green Zone where the conference was being held, the Iraqi army and the Americans were losing ground to local insurgent cells, which were recruiting young men on the premise of resisting America. Guerrilla war *was* spreading faster than an epidemic. Clean water did not stream from the tap. Sewage gushed onto the streets, and electricity was available for only a few hours a day. Reconstruction projects were halted because of constant security threats. These facts on the ground stood in the face of upbeat official analyses. In a period during which the newly trained Iraqi army was defecting in scores or being infiltrated by insurgents, forcing American officials to offer buyouts to suspects, the CPA spokesman Dan Senor told us, "Today in Iraq, there are more Iraqis in security forces, more Iraqis defending their own country than there are Americans in Iraq." While this may have been factually true, it deliberately missed the point: that we were losing the war. My translator asked me if I would use such a misleading quote, even though it was pure spin. I tried to give him a lesson in journalism, explaining the importance of allowing both sides to present their case and letting readers draw their own conclusions. I had to tell him that I had no choice but to quote the American officials, even if I knew that by doing so I would give their half-truths a measure of credibility.

In Iraq, two realities have always coexisted side by side. One reality is what journalists witness on the ground; the other is what American officials put forward in press briefings. Our professional training requires that we narrate both of these contending truths. As reporters, we need to give both sides equal weight and avoid personal opinions. Our conventional news stories, in which facts and quotes from both sides are layered in roughly equal measures, seldom make a big impact with an audience. It's not surprising that the stories that have gripped readers most have been first-person, opinionated dispatches, ones in which the reporter steps outside the objectivity bubble to offer a detailed contextual and emotional account of war. But the journalist who pens such stories risks being accused of bias, or worse, being deemed unfit to cover the war.

I had a taste of these swirling forces when a personal e-mail I sent to a group of friends was posted on the Internet and widely disseminated from there. In the dispatch, I was not being objective. I openly expressed my anger and frustration at the disastrous situation in Iraq. I criticized the rosy picture that administration officials painted for the American public. I concluded that Iraq was beyond salvation, and this sentence in particular, in the view of my critics, was deemed proof of my compromised professional ability to cover the war (despite the fact that a close inspection of my published work by *Wall Street Journal* editors proved no trace of bias and that then managing editor Paul Steiger issued a public statement supporting my professionalism). I often wonder, had I declared Iraq a resounding victory for U.S. forces, would my objectivity have been questioned? Would there have been calls for me to be reassigned because I was too optimistic?

Our news organizations have spent millions of dollars to maintain bureaus and correspondents in war zones. They, along with their personnel on the ground, take formidable risks to serve as the public's eyes and ears in Iraq. Yet it has taken almost five years for the American public to grasp the full scope of the disaster and reckon with their leaders' culpability in this military and human crisis. The question begs to be asked: Did the media get too caught up in the fog of war, or has the process of traditional news gathering, compounded with the pressures of loyalty to our nation and our troops, help contribute to a mangled portrait of the war?

Wars are decisive moments of truth. They expose the most elemental facts about human nature and the power of nations— from the true face of courage and tragedy to the military, technological, and diplomatic competence of feuding countries and their leaders.

The duty of a war reporter is to relay these truths from the front lines. The quality of such reporting underlines the process of national reckoning and self-examination that inevitably accompanies all wars. Truthful and accurate reporting can mean the difference between decisions made or deferred, actions ignored or boldly taken—and the lives that may be won or lost as a consequence.

The ultimate irony of the war in Iraq is that it is fought at a time when information is flowing around the globe more quickly and freely than ever, yet the American public has remained, for too long, isolated from the real scope of the disaster. It is an irony that certainly wouldn't be lost on George Orwell. To come to terms with the mistakes of our recent wars, and to draw the right conclusion from these events, Americans will need to reacquaint themselves with the facts. American journalism will also have to draw its own lessons about how well its corps is serving that goal.

Our Own Thought Police

MICHAEL MASSING

At first glance, the war in Iraq would seem to represent the realization of George Orwell's darkest fears. In "Politics and the English Language," he expressed alarm over how political speech and language, degraded by euphemism, vagueness, and cliché, was used to defend the indefensible, to make lies sound truthful and murder respectable. Three years later, in *1984*, Orwell offered an even grimmer vision, one in which an all-powerful Party, working through an all-seeing Ministry of Truth, manipulates and intimidates the public by pelting it with an endless series of distorted and fabricated messages. The Bush administration, in pushing for the war in Iraq, seems to have done much the same. It concocted lurid images to stir fear ("weapons of mass destruction," the prospect that the "smoking gun" could become a "mushroom cloud"). It asserted as fact information known to be false (the purported ties between Iraq and al Qaeda). It clipped and cropped intelligence data to fit its policy goals (dropping important qualifiers from the National Intelligence Estimate on Iraq). It worked up snippets and scraps of unsubstantiated evidence into a slick package of deception and misrepresentation

(Colin Powell's speech at the United Nations). And it created a whole glossary of diversionary terms—"preemptive war" for unprovoked aggression, "shock and awe" for a devastating bombing campaign, "coalition" for an invading force that was overwhelmingly American—all of which helped win the White House broad domestic support for a war that most of the rest of the world had decisively rejected.

Yet in many key respects, the Iraq war has diverged from Orwell's dystopic vision. Orwell had expected advances in technology to allow the ruling elite to monopolize the flow of information and through it to control the minds of the masses. In reality, though, those advances have set off an explosion in the number and diversity of news sources, making efforts at control all the harder to achieve. The twenty-four-hour cable news channels, the constantly updated news Web sites, news aggregators like Google News, post-it-yourself sites such as YouTube, e-zines, blogs, and digital cameras have all helped feed an avalanche of information about world affairs. In Iraq, reporters embedded with troops have been able via the Internet to file copy directly from the field. Through "milblogs," soldiers have been able to share with the outside world their impressions about their experiences on the ground. Even as the war has dragged on, it has given rise to a shelf-full of revealing books, written by not only generals and journalists but also captains, lieutenants, privates, national guardsmen, and even deserters.

In short, no war has been more fully chronicled or minutely analyzed than this one. And, as a result, the Bush administration has been unable to spin it as it would like. The spreading insurgency, the surging violence, the descent into chaos—all have been thoroughly documented by journalists and others, and public support for the war has steadily ebbed as a result.

Yet even amid this information glut, the public remains ill-informed about many key aspects of the war. This is due not to any restrictions imposed by the government, nor to any official management of language or image, but to controls imposed by the public itself. Americans—reluctant to confront certain raw realities of the war—have placed strong filters and screens on the facts and images they receive. This is particularly true regarding the conduct of U.S. troops in the field. The U.S. military in Iraq is an occupation army, and like most such forces, it has engaged in many troubling acts. With American men and women putting their lives at risk in a very hostile environment, however, the American public has little appetite for news about such acts, and so it sets limits on what it is willing to hear about them. The press—ever attuned to public sensitivities—will, on occasion, test those limits, but it generally respects them. The result is an unstated, unconscious, but nonetheless potent co-conspiracy between the public and the press to muffle some important truths about the war. In a disturbing twist on the Orwellian nightmare, the American people have become their own thought police, purging the news of unwanted and unwelcome features with an efficiency that government censors and military flacks can only envy.

Sometimes the public defines its limits by expressing outrage. The running of a story that seems too unsettling, or the airing of an image that seems too graphic, can set off a storm of protest—from Fox News and the *Weekly Standard*, bloggers and radio talk-show hosts, military families and enraged citizens—all denouncing the messenger as unpatriotic, un-American, even treasonous. In this swirl of menace and hate, even the most determined journalist can feel cowed.

Kevin Sites can attest to this. A freelance cameraman, Sites in November 2004 covered the second battle of Fallujah for

NBC News. On November 13, he followed a squad of Marines into a mosque that had been the scene of intense fighting. On the ground lay several badly wounded Iraqis. Seeing one of them move, a Marine shouted, "He's fucking faking he's dead," then shot him, making sure that he was. Sites caught the moment on tape and sent it to NBC. The network aired the clip but halted it at the moment when the soldier actually began firing. "NBC has chosen not to air the most gruesome of the images," anchor Brian Williams explained. Other networks did the same. (On the Arab satellite networks, the clip was shown in full, and repeatedly.) Even with this editing, Sites received thousands of death threats and pieces of hate mail. "Dear Liberal Media Scumbag," went one, "I hope the next video clip out of Iraq I watch is an insurgent placing your severed head onto your back." Bloggers accused him of being a traitor and an antiwar activist.

Since then, the networks have aired very few clips that approach even the truncated version of Sites's report. Sites himself no longer works for the networks; rather, he's out on his own, posting video reports from around the world on Yahoo.com, where his audience is a fraction of what it once was. To find truly revealing footage about the war, it's necessary to seek out documentaries such as *The Ground Truth* and *The War Tapes,* which play mainly before small elite audiences in art houses in the nation's largest cities.

In other cases, the public sets the limits of its tolerance through indifference and inattention, responding to reports of a shocking nature with a yawn and a sigh and thus causing these stories to wither and fade. The Haditha massacre is a good example. In March 2006, *Time* magazine reported that four months earlier, a group of Marines patrolling a remote village in western Iraq had lost one of its men to a roadside bomb. Furious, the soldiers had gone on a rampage, killing fifteen unarmed men, women, and children. Initially, the Marines involved in the attack claimed that the civilians had died from the insurgent bomb, and the military accepted their report. But *Time* had obtained a copy of a videotape of the attack's aftermath and, based on it, and on interviews with eyewitnesses, concluded that a massacre might have occurred. "What happened in Haditha," correspondent Tim McGirk wrote, "is a reminder of the horrors faced by civilians caught in the middle of war— and what war can do to the people who fight it."

All in all, it was an explosive report, presenting strong evidence of a Marine atrocity. Yet it stirred little public reaction, prompted no demands for an investigation, received scant follow-up from other news organizations. It was only two months later, when Congressman John Murtha denounced the slaughter at a press conference, declaring that the Marines had "killed innocent civilians in cold blood," that politicians began to pay attention to the episode, and that journalists began to write about it. Forced to investigate, the military determined that the Marines had killed not fifteen but twenty-four civilians, and it initiated proceedings against eight of the soldiers.

From that point on, the massacre—validated as newsworthy by a leading congressman—received extensive coverage. Even so, it was framed as a rare exception, as an aberration from the otherwise commendable behavior of U.S. soldiers in Iraq. But, as William Langewiesche found in an investigation for *Vanity Fair*, the incident was not all that exceptional. The initial failure of the Marines to fully investigate the killings was due not to any conspiracy or cover-up but to the fact that the bloodshed was not regarded as anything out of the ordinary. "The killing of civilians," Langewiesche wrote, "has become so common-place that the report of these particular ones barely aroused no-tice as it moved up the chain of command in Iraq." The debacle in Haditha grew out of the "normal operations in the war," he observed, operations that "make such carnage routine."

Few other publications, however, were willing to explore this. Doing so would require acknowledging that U.S. soldiers in Iraq are not necessarily paragons of virtue, that they do not al-ways show respect for Iraqi civilians, that at times they harass, abuse, injure, and even kill them. It would require acknowledg-ing that the Iraq war, like most wars, is a savage, pitiless affair in which American soldiers have been forced to do many un-American things. Most Americans prefer not to confront this. They want to be able to maintain their belief that Americans are an exceptionally virtuous, freedom-loving people and that their soldiers are a uniquely compassionate, well-meaning force. Any assertions to the contrary can rouse the beast, and the press, well aware of this, tends to tread warily around it.

Needless to say, many U.S. soldiers do behave in an upright fashion. Intent on doing good, they have distributed toys to children, cleaned up streets in poor neighborhoods, and arranged medical help for the injured and ailing. But these sol-diers have been placed in an extraordinarily perilous environ-ment with minimal preparation, and as the security situation has deteriorated and the population has grown increasingly bel-ligerent, they have responded in ways that do not always con-form to the standards taught in army field manuals.

For a truly unsanitized look at the nature of the occupation, one must consult the many books that have been written about it. Just as the most graphic footage from Iraq has been tucked away in documentaries, so has the rawest reporting been relegated to books that only the most motivated will seek out. Especially revealing are the many firsthand accounts produced by ordinary soldiers. Among them are *My War: Killing Time in Iraq*, by Colby Buzzell, a pot-smoking admirer of Charles Bukowski, Ralph Nader, and George Orwell and the operator of one of the most widely read milblogs (until it was shut down by the military); *Love My Rifle More than You: Young and Female in the U.S. Army*, by Kayla Williams, a freewheeling, foulmouthed military intelligence specialist; *The Deserter's Tale*, by Joshua Key, a private from Oklahoma who, appalled by the brutality and cruelty of his fellow soldiers, left his unit and fled to Canada; and *Operation Homecoming*, a collection of eyewitness accounts, private journals, and short stories by U.S. soldiers sponsored by the National Endowment for the Arts. In these books are recorded not only many acts of courage, self-sacrifice, and benevolence but also many deeply disturbing aspects of the U.S. presence in Iraq—realities that tend to get airbrushed out of news accounts. Among them:

- The prevalence of drug use among U.S. troops. From these books, it seems clear that heavy drinking, hash smoking, and pill popping (especially of Valium, which is widely available in Iraq) are commonplace among U.S. soldiers in Iraq. Near universal is the use of "dip," or smokeless tobacco, which causes soldiers to spit out thick gobs of brown goo everywhere they go.

- The ubiquity of pornography. Before the invasion, porn was all but unavailable in Iraq, but the presence of 130,000 U.S. troops has helped create an active market in it. Many Iraqis have since developed a taste for it as well, and soldiers freely trade porn for alcohol and pills. They also use it to motivate their Iraqi counterparts, promising a peek at a skin magazine in return for their going out on patrol.

• The frequency of stealing from Iraqis. Despite strict prohibitions against this, U.S. soldiers on raids or at checkpoints sometimes unburden Iraqis of cash, jewelry, knives, electronic equipment, and sunglasses. Cars and motorcycles are sometimes seized as well.

• The widespread contempt in which Iraqis are held. This is evident in the lexicon of racially charged terms used to refer to them: ragheads, camel jockeys, sand niggers, terrorists, and "the fucking locals." Many soldiers come to regard Arabs as "smelly, awful people," Kayla Williams writes. The labels for Iraqis are but a subset of the raw, thoroughly profane language many soldiers in Iraq use, a trait that generally goes unmentioned in journalistic reports from the field.

• The routine mistreatment of Iraqi citizens during house raids. U.S. forces have undertaken thousands of these actions, hoping to find insurgents, weapons, and intelligence. In carrying them out, they often break down doors, bust up furniture, rip up mattresses, round up sleeping children from their beds, and arrest and zipcuff every able-bodied male in sight. These men are frequently punched, kicked, burned with cigarettes, and generally roughed up. In these books, a Marine brags of punching prisoners in the face or groin when no one is looking; a detainee is repeatedly kicked in the face in an effort to make him stop laughing; a prisoner suffers a broken jaw; another dies in custody. The vast majority of those detained turn out to be innocent. From these accounts, it seems clear that the types of abuses committed at Abu Ghraib were not the work of "a few bad apples," as most Americans insist on believing, but common occurrences throughout the archipelago of detention facilities maintained by the United States in Iraq.

- The killing of innocent Iraqis at checkpoints. Throughout Iraq, U.S. soldiers set up roadblocks to check for weapons and prevent car bombs, but the sites are often so poorly marked that Iraqis do not realize that they are supposed to stop at them. When they fail to do so, they are often fired on and not infrequently killed. These books are filled with gruesome accounts in which U.S. soldiers, worried that they were coming under attack, gunned down innocent Iraqis.

- The high civilian death toll in Iraq. Checkpoints are but one type of encounter in which innocent Iraqis die at the hands of U.S. soldiers. Convoys of U.S. military vehicles frequently run Iraqi cars off the road, causing injury and sometimes death. U.S. soldiers, when shot at, routinely respond by opening up fire and pumping round after indiscriminate round into hamlets, towns, and urban neighborhoods. When a location is suspected of harboring insurgents, it is often pounded by artillery rounds or air strikes, with often devastating results for civilians. In *The Deserter's Tale*, Joshua Key observes that each military company in Iraq is responsible for dealing with the bodies of the civilians it has killed, and it fell to him to build a shack to hold the bodies of Iraqis slain by his unit until someone came to claim them.

In contrast to the deaths from car bombs and suicide attacks of the insurgents, most of the civilian deaths caused by Americans are unintentional. That does not, however, make them any less wrenching for the victims and their families. In the Arab news media, this ongoing slaughter receives constant coverage. In the American media, it receives very little. One can watch the evening news shows for nights on end, one can scour U.S. papers week after week and not find any acknowledgment of the many civilians who have been killed by GIs. Writing in the *Washington Post* in July 2006, Andrew J. Bacevich, a professor of international relations at Boston University and the author of two highly regarded studies of U.S. foreign policy, expressed dismay at the indifference shown by both the military and the American public toward the ongoing slaughter of Iraqi noncombatants by U.S. soldiers. Observing that nobody has even bothered to keep a tally of the victims, Bacevich surmised from his own readings that the number "almost certainly runs in the tens of thousands." Aside from the obvious moral questions this raises, he went on, the violence against civilians has undermined America's policies in Iraq and the Mideast generally by "suggesting to Iraqis and Americans alike that Iraqi civilians—and perhaps Arabs and Muslims more generally—are expendable."

How can such a critical feature of the U.S. occupation remain so hidden from view? Because most Americans don't want to know about it. The books by Iraqi vets are filled with expressions of disbelief and rage at the lack of interest ordinary

Americans show for what they've had to endure on the battle-field. In *Operation Homecoming*, one returning Marine, who takes to drinking heavily in an effort to cope with the crushing guilt and revulsion he feels over how many people he's seen killed, fumes about how "you can't talk to them [ordinary Americans] about the horror of a dead child's lifeless mutilated body staring back at you from the void, knowing you took part in that end." Writing of her return home, Kayla Williams notes that the things most people seemed interested in were "beyond my comprehension. Who cared about Jennifer Lopez? How was it that I was watching CNN one morning and there was a story about freaking ducklings being fished out of a damn sewer drain—while the story of soldiers getting killed in Iraq got relegated to this little banner across the bottom of the screen?" In *Generation Kill*, by the journalist Evan Wright, a Marine corporal confides his anguish and anger over all the killings he has seen: "I think it's bullshit how these fucking civilians are dying! They're worse off than the guys that are shooting at us. They don't even have a chance. Do you think people at home are going to see this—all these women and children we're killing? Fuck no. Back home they're glorifying this motherfucker, I guarantee you."

Generation Kill recounts Wright's experiences traveling with a Marine platoon during the initial invasion. The platoon was at the very tip of the spear of the invasion force, and Wright got a uniquely close-up view of the fighting. In most U.S. news accounts, the invasion was portrayed as a relatively bloodless affair, with few American casualties and not many more civilian ones. Wright offers a starkly different tale. While expressing admiration for the Marines' many acts of valor and displays of compassion, he marvels at the U.S. military's ferocious firepower and shudders at the startling number of civilians who fell victim to it. He writes of neighborhoods being leveled by mortar rounds, of villages being flattened by air strikes, of innocent men, women, and children being mowed down in free-fire zones. At first, Wright notes, the Marines found it easy, even exciting, to kill, but as the invasion progressed and the civilian toll mounted, many began to recoil, and some even broke down. "Do you realize the shit we've done here, the people we've killed?" one Marine agonizes. "Back home in the civilian world, if we did this, we would go to prison."

In an interview he gave soon after the publication of his book, Wright said that his main aim in writing it was to deglamorize the war—and war in general. The problem with American society, he said, "is we don't really understand what war is. Our understanding of it is too sanitized." For the past decade, he explained, "we've been steeped in the lore of *The Greatest Generation*"—Tom Brokaw's book about the men who fought in World War II—"and a lot of people have developed this romanticism about that war. They tend to remember it from the *Life* magazine images of the sailor coming home and kissing his fiancée. They've forgotten that war is about killing." In *Generation Kill*, he noted, he wanted to show how soldiers kill and wound civilians. In some cases, he said, the U.S. military justified such killings by the presence of Iraqi Fedayeen fighters among the civilian population, but, he added, "when you see a little girl in pretty clothes that someone dressed her in, and she's smushed on the road with her legs cut off, you don't think, 'Well, you know, there were Fedayeen nearby and this is collateral damage. They're just civilians.'" The "real rule of war that you learn—and this was true in World War II—is that people who suffer the most are civilians," Wright said.

"You're safest if you're a soldier. I'm haunted by the images of people that I saw killed by my country."

As Wright suggests, the sanitizing of news in wartime is nothing new. In most wars, nations that send their men and women off to fight in distant lands don't want to learn too much about the violence being committed in their name. Facing up to this would cause too much shame, would deal too great a blow to national self-esteem. If people were to become too aware of the butchery wars entail, they would become much less willing to fight them. And so the illusion must be maintained that war is a noble enterprise, that the soldiers who wage it are full of valor and heroism, that in the end their intentions are good and their actions benign.

In his reflections on politics and language, Orwell operated on the assumption that people want to know the truth. Often, though, they don't. In the case of Iraq, the many instruments Orwell felt would be needed to keep people passive and uninformed—the nonstop propaganda messages, the memory holes, the rewriting of history, Room 101—have proved unnecessary. The public has become its own collective Ministry of Truth—a reality that, in many ways, is even more chilling than the one Orwell envisioned.

What I Didn't Know:
Open Society Reconsidered

GEORGE SOROS

In his novel *1984*, George Orwell gave a chilling description of a totalitarian regime in which all means of communication are controlled by a Ministry of Truth and dissidents are persecuted by the political police. Orwell wrote the book as a warning that the whole world could turn into the Soviet system of the time. Obviously, the threat did not materialize. The United States remains a democracy governed by a constitution and by the rule of law, with a pluralistic media. Yet there are some disturbing signs that the propaganda methods Orwell describes in his novel have taken root in contemporary America.

What I find most troubling is that the American people seem so susceptible to manipulation. The outstanding example is the War on Terror, which has imposed a false and misleading interpretation of the threat presented by the terrorist attack of 9/11. The general public has bought into that interpretation so completely that even though it criticizes the war in Iraq, it is loath to challenge the War on Terror as a false metaphor. This is not the only case where public opinion has been successfully manipulated. Political discourse is rife with examples: the Clear Skies Act actually relaxes the rules on air pollution; the Healthy Forest Restoration Act actually permits clear-cutting; and the No Child Left Behind Act imposes testing standards without providing the necessary funds. Needless to say, both sides of American politics engage in deliberate deception at election time.

How could propaganda methods reminiscent of Orwell's worst fears prove so successful in contemporary America? How could the public be so badly misled?

My own answer goes right to the heart of the concept of an open society. I shall argue that open societies in which various ideas compete for acceptance are just as susceptible to deliberate deception as are closed societies, where a particular ideology enjoys a monopoly. We cannot protect ourselves against false metaphors and other techniques of deception unless we reaffirm our commitment to understanding reality. But that is not as simple as it sounds. Why should we bother with understanding reality when reality can be so easily manipulated? To answer this question in the affirmative, we need to reexamine the relationship between our ideas and reality. This mental exercise will lead to a reformulation of the concept of open society. I will need to take the reader through this exercise even at the cost of getting embroiled in a somewhat dense philosophical argument. I apologize in advance.

As conscious beings, we seek to understand and form a view of the world in which we live. Let's call this pursuit of knowledge the *cognitive function* of the mind. Cognition is necessary if we want to make an impact on the world, so that it will correspond to our desires. I used to think of the latter as the participating function, but for the purposes of this argument, I should like to rename it the *manipulating function*. The need to at once comprehend and influence reality is the task that confronts us as thinking agents.

The two functions—cognitive and manipulative, knowledge-seeking and reality-influencing—go hand in hand, but they work in opposite directions. The cognitive function takes a situation as given and seeks to form a view that corresponds to it. The manipulating function takes desires as given and seeks to make situations correspond to them. In an imaginary world, where the two functions can always be isolated from each other, both could work perfectly: People's views could correspond to reality and the consequences of their actions could correspond to their expectations. But that is not the world in which we live. People perform both functions at the same time, and since the two work in opposite directions, they can interfere with each other. I call this interference *reflexivity*. Reflexivity explains why our understanding is imperfect and why our actions have unintended consequences.

The feedback loop of reflexivity affects only a relatively narrow segment of reality. In the realm of natural phenomena, events occur independently of what anybody thinks; therefore, natural science can explain and predict the course of events with reasonable accuracy. Reflexivity is confined to social phenomena, but where it is present, it introduces an element of uncertainty both into our understanding and into the actual course of events. Consider the statement "It is raining." It is either true or false, depending on whether it is, in fact, raining. Now consider the statement "You are my enemy." That may be both true and false, depending, among other things, on your reaction.

Uncertainty is difficult to live with. We need to know what is true and what is false, what is right and what is wrong, in order to make decisions. There are two ways to deal with uncertainty. One is to embrace ideologies and religious belief systems that lay claim to some ultimate truth. The other is to act on a set of beliefs, knowing that we may be wrong. The latter is much harder to cope with. Dogmatic ideologies remove doubt, but they have a major drawback: They are bound to be false. They can be imposed on society only by repressive methods that stifle free discussion and prevent a better understanding of reality. Such ideologies lead to a closed society. By contrast, open society is based on the recognition that our understanding is inherently imperfect. Although this insight forces us to live with uncertainty, it also allows us to get closer to reality through a critical process of trial and error. The positive results of the critical process may be sufficient to compensate for the hardships connected with uncertainty. When that is the case, open societies are able to resist the temptations of totalitarian ideologies.

The United States is an open society, but people are not widely familiar with the idea. The Constitution of the United States predated by a century and a half the philosophical concept of open society. The founding fathers drew their inspiration directly from the Enlightenment. The philosophers of the Enlightenment put their faith in reason, expecting it to provide a full and accurate picture of reality. Reason was supposed to work like a searchlight, illuminating a reality that lay passively, awaiting discovery. The possibility that the decisions of thinking agents could influence the situation was left out of the account. The Enlightenment failed to recognize reflexivity. It postulated an imaginary world in which the manipulating function could not interfere with the cognitive function. This resulted in a distorted view of reality, but one that was appropriate to an age when so many things were waiting to be discovered and so many exciting discoveries were in fact made. Although the faith in reason was not fully justified, it produced truly impressive results, which were sufficient to sustain the Enlightenment for two centuries. The ideas of the Enlightenment have become deeply ingrained in Western civilization.

Ideas that do not fully correspond to reality but nevertheless produce positive results have played an important role in history. I call them "fertile fallacies." I would go so far as to claim that all civilizations are based on fertile fallacies. The Enlightenment is a prime example. It ignored reflexivity, but it produced the Constitution of the United States and the Bill of Rights, which are among the greatest achievements of our civilization. These documents assert the greatest degree of individual freedom compatible with the freedom of others. But the underlying assumption—that freedom of thought and speech will assure that reason will prevail—is incorrect.

Where exactly is the fallacy in the Enlightenment? It lies in separating reason from reality. Although the philosophers of the Enlightenment understood the role of the will and emotion, they gave precedence to the cognitive function over the manipulating function. The Enlightenment fallacy is an obvious one to fall into. We need to keep our thinking separate from the subject matter that we think about to be able to formulate factually correct statements, and we must give precedence to the cognitive function over the manipulating function if we are interested in pursuing knowledge. The separation of reason and reality is deeply rooted in Western philosophy. Nevertheless, it contains a fallacy. It is appropriate to the realm of natural science, where reason is, in fact, separated from reality, and events occur independently of what anybody thinks. It is misleading in social science, where the participants' thinking forms part of the reality that scientists seek to study. And it is downright false in politics, where the manipulating function prevails over the cognitive.

In the realm of natural science, facts and statements genuinely belong to separate universes. That is why scientists have been so successful in establishing theories that correspond to the facts. In the realm of social science, the separation is less clear-cut because thoughts and statements form part of the subject matter. Medicine is on the border between natural and social science. In social science, theories may influence the facts. This makes it harder to understand reality, while opening a loophole for manipulating reality. To take advantage of the loophole, social theories need to at least pretend that they serve the cognitive function in order to benefit from the reputation that scientific method has achieved. Marxism serves as the prime example. Karl Popper exposed Marx by showing that Marxism does not qualify as scientific because the theory cannot be falsified. As I have tried to show elsewhere (*The Alchemy of Finance*, 1987), the same argument applies to the notion that markets always tend toward equilibrium. I call that notion "market fundamentalism" and I consider it just as tendentious and manipulative as Marxism.

Natural scientists may wish to manipulate reality so as to make it conform to their desires, but they cannot get away with it. That is why they have to go through the laborious process of first gaining knowledge and then applying it, in order to bring about the desired results. In politics, by contrast, the desired results can be brought about more directly by manipulating people's perceptions and, if necessary, deliberately deceiving them. Politicians are likely to give precedence to the manipulating function because their chances of getting elected and staying in power depend on it. Once they are in power, the cognitive function assumes greater importance, because that determines to what extent their policies will produce desired outcomes. But those who give precedence to the cognitive function at all times are unlikely to attain and occupy positions of power.

The achievements of natural science fascinated philosophers and led to the logical positivist school, which asserted that statements whose truth or validity cannot be determined by an appeal to the facts are meaningless. This idea, of course, is false because the subjective views of participants—which by definition do not correspond to the facts—can objectively alter the situations to which they refer.

Karl Popper was a trenchant critic of logical positivism, yet he, too, bought into the idea that the purpose of critical thinking is to gain a better understanding of reality. Until quite recently, I was too much under Popper's influence to recognize the error in this assumption. I did not realize that in political discourse the cognitive function takes precedence over the manipulating function. That insight came to me when I asked myself the question: How could the Bush administration mislead the American public so badly?

My failure to recognize that political discourse is dominated by the manipulating function is a glaring example of the sway that the Enlightenment fallacy holds over our thinking. After all, I arrived at the concept of reflexivity nearly fifty years ago, yet I continued to be guided by Popper's concept of open society. I now recognize that the purpose of political discourse in a democracy is to get elected and stay in power. Those who think that democratic debate primarily serves the cognitive function are victims of the Enlightenment fallacy. In his 1946 essay "Politics and the English Language," Orwell inveighed against the abuse of language in service of the manipulating function—a concept he did not recognize, but the workings of which he understood all too well. Orwell meant *1984* to serve as a terrifying example, and his essay "Politics and the English Language" as a lesson for future generations. It is ironic that today his seminal essay is largely ignored and *1984* is used as a textbook by unscrupulous manipulators such as Republican consultant Frank Luntz, who claims credit for many of the most successful deceptions practiced by the radical right in America.

THE TENDENCY TO MANIPULATE public opinion is not peculiar to contemporary America. It is innate to the political process. It prevails both in open and closed societies, although the methods and institutions are liable to be different. Yet the present situation in America is unique. It is both different and more dangerous than in the past. The techniques of deception have undergone enormous improvements since Orwell's time. Many of these techniques were developed in connection with the advertising and marketing of commercial products and services, and then adapted to politics. Their distinguishing feature is that they can be bought for money. More recently, cognitive science has helped to make the techniques of deception even more effective.

The findings of cognitive science demonstrate that the disembodied intellect, or reason as something separate from reality, is a figment of our imagination. Reason is inextricably intertwined with emotion. Moreover, emotions can be activated without engaging consciousness because only a small proportion of mental processes ever enter into consciousness. Negative and positive emotions involve different neural circuits, and the two are not directly connected, so they can be independently influenced.[1] Television connects with the emotions more directly than the printed word. Seeing something on television activates the same neural networks as experiencing that same thing directly.

Television and cognitive science combined have enabled political operatives to arouse emotions in ways that bypass conscious judgment.[2] The fact that people can be successfully manipulated has given rise to political professionals not bound by the Enlightenment fallacy, and they concentrate only on getting results. They utilize the findings of cognitive science and appeal primarily to emotions rather than reason. In politics, such men and women have found a home on the radical right because the political establishment was too hamstrung by the Enlightenment fallacy. In this way, the radical right stole a march on more traditionally minded politicians and political professionals. First, they captured the Republican Party, and then, using the terrorist attack of 9/11 as a pretext, took over most levers of power. Both Republicans and Democrats engage in deliberate deception, but the radical right has been more successful, partly because it is not hindered by the Enlightenment fallacy and partly because it has been better financed. We have witnessed the rise of professional dishonesty: People whose job it is to manipulate reality can take professional pride in their accomplishments. Moreover, they are liable to enjoy the respect of an American public that admires success no matter how it is achieved. The fact that professional dishonesty has become respectable casts doubt on the concept of open society as it was formulated by Karl Popper and later adopted by others, including me. This adds urgency to the reexamination.

Open society is based on the recognition that perfect knowledge is unattainable, but we can gain a better understanding of reality by engaging in critical thinking. Under the influence of the Enlightenment fallacy, proponents of open society failed to recognize that in politics, gathering public support takes precedence over the pursuit of truth. As a result, the democratic debate does not necessarily lead to a better understanding of reality.

This insight should lead us not to abandon the concept of open society, but to revise and reaffirm the case for it. The revision consists in abandoning the tacit assumption that political discourse aims at a better understanding of reality and reintroducing it as an explicit requirement. This means that open society cannot be ensured merely by the division of powers, free speech, and free elections; it also requires a commitment to the pursuit of truth.

Understanding reality is a social enterprise that requires all the participants to abide by certain ground rules. The scientific method provides the most successful example of this. To conduct successful tests requires an agreement on principles, such as the requirement that scientific experiments have to be replicable. The ground rules for political discourse cannot be identical to scientific method, but they should be similar in character: They should constitute socially accepted values such as truthfulness and respect for other people's opinions. Why should politicians bother with understanding reality when it can be so easily manipulated? Only because the public cares about the truth and punishes politicians when it catches them in deliberate deception. And why should the public care? Because the misinterpretation of reality produces negative results. Politics is about the pursuit of power, not the pursuit of truth. Nevertheless, the truth matters because deception misleads people in choosing their representatives, distorts policy choices and the execution of policies, interferes with holding politicians accountable, and destroys trust in democracy.

Recent history provides convincing evidence that if you engage in policies based on a misrepresentation of reality, reality is liable to catch up with you. That is what happened after 9/11—not because of the terrorist attack, but because of the way the Bush administration responded to it, declaring a War on Terror and treating any criticism as unpatriotic. This smoke screen allowed the Bush administration to invade Iraq on false pretenses, violate human rights on a large scale, abandon the Geneva Conventions and habeas corpus, restrict civil liberties, and extend executive powers beyond the limits envisioned by the Constitution. The results have been disastrous.

The public is now awakening, as if from a bad dream. What can we learn from the experience? The importance of the critical process that is the hallmark of open society has, in fact, been reaffirmed. Open society remains preferable to a dictatorship or the rule of a philosopher king, not because an electorate that is constantly bombarded by misleading messages is a better judge of reality than a philosopher king, but because the electorate is in a better position to correct the mistakes of the rulers than the rulers themselves. It takes time for a divergence between outcomes and expectations to become apparent, but once it does, the electorate can replace the rulers.

What we have learned—what we should have known—is that the supremacy of the cognitive function in political discourse cannot be taken for granted. It can be ensured only by an electorate that respects reality and punishes politicians who lie or engage in other forms of deception.

The concept of open society I am proposing here differs in an important respect from the one I inherited from Karl Popper. Popper took the supremacy of the cognitive function for granted. I now recognize that assumption was false: In political discourse, the manipulative function takes precedence. That implicit assumption has to be replaced by an explicit requirement that people respect reality and hold politicians accountable. This requirement is *additional* to the various freedoms with which open society has been traditionally associated. Without a commitment to the cognitive function, the critical process that Karl Popper extolled will not produce the desired results.

That commitment is all the more difficult to make now that we know that reality can be manipulated. This poses a twofold obstacle to the pursuit of cognition. First, reality becomes more difficult to understand because it constitutes a moving target: All the tendentious and biased interpretations of reality make an impact on the reality that needs to be understood. Second, the rules and conventions that work so well in science do not carry the same weight in political discourse because the participants are more interested in manipulating reality in their favor than in understanding it. Nevertheless, the importance of the cognitive function needs to be reaffirmed because the misinterpretation of reality is bound to bring unintended adverse consequences. What better time to bring this argument home than the present, when the unintended adverse consequences of the War on Terror are so clearly visible?

How can the cognitive function be given more weight when the political discourse is dominated by the manipulating function? When politicians distort reality, the electorate ought to punish them for it by voting them out of power. If the electorate were committed to a better understanding of reality, political professionals would learn to give it more weight. The practical difficulty is in recognizing when the political professionals are distorting reality. There is an important role here for the media, the political elite, and the educational system, which must all act responsibly in their commitment to the principles of open society. They have to act as watchdogs protecting a less well-informed and more gullible public.

WHAT CAN A RESPONSIBLE MEDIA and a committed educated elite do to protect the public from deliberate deception? The public needs to be inoculated against the various techniques of deception by being made aware of them. The most effective techniques operate at the subconscious level. When emotions can be aroused by methods that bypass consciousness, the public is left largely defenseless. But if the public is made aware of the various techniques, it is likely to reject them.

There is much to be learned from recent experience. When I heard President Bush warning that people who do not support his policies are supporting the terrorists, I heard alarm bells ringing. I had been exposed to Nazi and Communist propaganda in my youth, and I knew the warning signs. The American public did not share my alarm because it had not been exposed to similar manipulation before. But now that Americans have had the experience and have seen the results, they ought to have an allergic reaction when they are exposed to similar methods.

My personal experience has given me the opportunity to study the process up close. When I took an active role in opposing President Bush's 2004 reelection, I was subjected to a concerted campaign of personal vilification. The attack was led by the Republican National Committee, which sent out regular mass mailings making various unflattering and untrue allegations about me. These were then amplified by *The O'Reilly Factor,* Rush Limbaugh, the editorial page of the *Wall Street Journal,* and the *New York Post,* among others. Feeding into these channels was a nebulous opposition research network financed by the Pittsburgh billionaire Richard Mellon Scaife. It was the same shadowy network that persecuted the Clintons when they were in the White House and finally succeeded in entrapping President Clinton in a perjury. The campaign recently gained new momentum when two operatives, David Horowitz and Richard Poe, published a book entitled *The Shadow Party: How George Soros, Hillary Clinton, and Sixties Radicals Seized Control of the Democratic Party,* and when Bill O'Reilly devoted a chapter to me in his book *Culture Warrior* and featured me prominently in his shows.

This campaign painted a totally false and misleading picture of me. I was allegedly a Nazi collaborator in World War II; I was said to have profited from my foundations in Russia; I was the Lenin of an anti-American conspiracy, to mention only the most blatant lies. I was defenseless against these accusations. There were no legal remedies available, and to contest the allegations publicly would have merely rewarded my attackers by drawing attention to their spurious campaign. But the experience allowed me to witness their manipulative methods firsthand. As the attacks went on, I could identify a number of recurring deceptive devices and rhetorical techniques, including:

1. *Conflating facts and opinions:* The writer gives a reasonably factual account and then introduces an opinion as if it were a fact. Someone who disagrees with this opinion can then be accused of deliberately and knowingly falsifying facts.

2. *Guilt by association:* The writer establishes ties, however tenuous, between the object of attack and others, and holds the object of attack responsible for the behavior of others.

3. *Conspiracy theory:* The writer assumes that everyone who is mentioned is acting in concert.

4. *Mixing sources:* The writer quotes a number of reliable sources and then mixes in some products of "opposition research," giving the impression that they are equally reliable.

5. *Transference:* The writer accuses his opponent of having the same motives or using the same techniques that he has or uses himself.

6. *False labeling:* The writer divides the world between us and them, good and bad, left and right, and then condemns people by labeling them.

7. *False patriotism:* The writer accuses the opponent of being unpatriotic and anti-American.

Perhaps the most influential of these devices is what I have called transference: accusing your opponent of having the same motives or using the same techniques as you. It is the key to O'Reilly's book. He claims to be a conservative who is trying to defend America against the incursions of what he calls "Secular Progressives." In fact, he is a radical who is trying to overturn the secular tradition, which is enshrined in the Constitution. Similarly, the authors of *The Shadow Party* transfer to the Democratic Party one of the defining qualities of Republicans: The Democrats are depicted as having been hijacked by the well-funded advocates of a radical ideology. It is relevant that David Horowitz, who accuses me of being "the Lenin of the anti-American conspiracy," used to be a Trotskyite. Similarly, Ann Coulter's last bestseller, *Godless,* transfers her own brand of religion to the liberals when she speaks of the "Church of Liberalism."

Propaganda often goes beyond transference by completely reversing meanings and turning reality on its head. That is what Fox News does when it calls itself "fair and balanced" and what the Bush administration does when it uses names like the "Clear Skies Act" and the "No Child Left Behind Act." Republican pollster Frank Luntz says that he learned the technique from George Orwell, so it would be appropriate to call it Newspeak. Karl Rove and his acolytes have carried the Orwellian technique even further by selecting their opponents' strongest traits and treating them as their Achilles' heels, using insinuations as well as bold-faced lies. Their goal is to portray opponent achievements as phony. That is how they defeated Vietnam War veterans Senator Max Cleland in 2002 and John Kerry in 2004.

The common feature of these Newspeak devices is their total disregard for reality. A false picture of reality is driven into people's consciousness through constant repetition. A whole network of publications is devoted to the task, some of which manage to parade as mainstream media. These deceptive practices have come increasingly to dominate the American political discourse, particularly in paid political announcements. Both sides use them, but the radical right has been more effective.

The general public has proven to be remarkably susceptible to the manipulation of truth, yet I believe it may be possible to inoculate the public against false arguments by arousing resentment against being manipulated. This could be served by identifying the techniques of manipulation and naming them when they are used. In 1980, Ronald Reagan scored big against Jimmy Carter in the second presidential debate just by saying, "There you go again." Perhaps the same result could be achieved if we said, "There you go again" every time an Orwellian Newspeak technique is used.

Politics and the English Language

GEORGE ORWELL

Most people who bother with the matter at all would admit that the English language is in a bad way, but it is generally assumed that we cannot by conscious action do anything about it. Our civilization is decadent and our language—so the argument runs—must inevitably share in the general collapse. It follows that any struggle against the abuse of language is a sentimental archaism, like preferring candles to electric light or hansom cabs to aeroplanes. Underneath this lies the half-conscious belief that language is a natural growth and not an instrument which we shape for our own purposes.

Now, it is clear that the decline of a language must ultimately have political and economic causes: it is not due simply to the bad influence of this or that individual writer. But an effect can become a cause, reinforcing the original cause and producing the same effect in an intensified form, and so on indefinitely. A man may take to drink because he feels himself to be a failure, and then fail all the more completely because he drinks. It is rather the same thing that is happening to the English language. It becomes ugly and inaccurate because our thoughts are foolish, but the slovenliness of our language makes it easier for us to have foolish thoughts. The point is that the process is reversible. Modern English, especially written English, is full of bad habits which spread by imitation and which can be avoided if one is willing to take the necessary trouble. If one gets rid of these habits one can think more clearly, and to think clearly is a necessary first step towards political regeneration: so that the fight against bad English is not frivolous and is not the exclusive concern of professional writers. I will come back to this presently, and I hope that by that time the meaning of what I have said here will have become clearer. Meanwhile, here are five specimens of the English language as it is now habitually written.

These five passages have not been picked out because they are especially bad—I could have quoted far worse if I had chosen—but because they illustrate various of the mental vices from which we now suffer. They are a little below the average, but are fairly representative samples. I number them so that I can refer back to them when necessary:

1. I am not, indeed, sure whether it is not true to say that the Milton who once seemed not unlike a seventeenth-century Shelley had not become, out of an experience ever more bitter in each year, more alien [*sic*] to the founder of that Jesuit sect which nothing could induce him to tolerate.
   —**Professor Harold Laski**
   (Essay in *Freedom of Expression*).

2. Above all, we cannot play ducks and drakes with a native battery of idioms which prescribes such egregious collocations of vocables as the Basic *put up with* for *tolerate* or *put at a loss* for *bewilder*.
   —Professor Lancelot Hogben
   (*Interglossa*).

3. On the one side we have the free personality: by definition it is not neurotic, for it has neither conflict nor dream. Its desires, such as they are, are transparent, for they are just what institutional approval keeps in the forefront of consciousness; another institutional pattern would alter their number and intensity; there is little in them that is natural, irreducible, or culturally dangerous. But *on the other side*, the social bond itself is nothing but the mutual reflection of these self-secure integrities. Recall the definition of love. Is not this the very picture of a small academic? Where is there a place in this hall of mirrors for either personality or fraternity?
   —Essay on psychology in *Politics* (New York).

4. All the "best people" from the gentlemen's clubs, and all the frantic fascist captains, united in common hatred of Socialism and bestial horror of the rising tide of the mass revolutionary movement, have turned to acts of provocation, to foul incendiarism, to medieval legends of poisoned wells, to legalize their own destruction of proletarian organizations, and rouse the agitated petty-bourgeoisie to chauvinistic fervor on behalf of the fight against the revolutionary way out of the crisis.
   —Communist pamphlet.

5. If a new spirit *is* to be infused into this old country, there is one thorny and contentious reform which must be tackled, and that is the humanization and galvanization of the B.B.C. Timidity here will bespeak canker and atrophy of the soul. The heart of Britain may be sound and of strong beat, for instance, but the British lion's roar at present is like that of Bottom in Shakespeare's *Midsummer Night's Dream*—as gentle as any sucking dove. A virile new Britain cannot continue indefinitely to be traduced in the eyes, or rather ears, of the world by the effete languors of Langham Place, brazenly masquerading as "standard English." When the Voice of Britain is heard at nine o'clock, better far and infinitely less ludicrous to hear aitches honestly dropped than the present priggish, inflated, inhibited, school-ma'amish arch braying of blameless bashful mewing maidens!

— Letter in *Tribune*

Each of these passages has faults of its own, but, quite apart from avoidable ugliness, two qualities are common to all of them. The first is staleness of imagery; the other is lack of precision. The writer either has a meaning and cannot express it, or he inadvertently says something else, or he is almost indifferent as to whether his words mean anything or not. This mixture of vagueness and sheer incompetence is the most marked characteristic of modern English prose, and especially of any kind of political writing. As soon as certain topics are raised, the concrete melts into the abstract and no one seems able to think of turns of speech that are not hackneyed: prose consists less and less of *words* chosen for the sake of their meaning, and more and more of *phrases* tacked together like the sections of a prefabricated hen-house. I list below, with notes and examples, various of the tricks by means of which the work of prose-construction is habitually dodged:

DYING METAPHORS. A newly invented metaphor assists thought by evoking a visual image, while on the other hand a metaphor which is technically "dead" (e.g. *iron resolution*) has in effect reverted to being an ordinary word and can generally be used without loss of vividness. But in between these two classes there is a huge dump of worn-out metaphors which have lost all evocative power and are merely used because they save people the trouble of inventing phases for themselves. Examples are: *Ring the changes on, take up the cudgels for, toe the line, ride roughshod over, stand shoulder to shoulder with, play into the hands of, no axe to grind, grist to the mill, fishing in troubled waters, on the order of the day, Achilles' heel, swan song, hotbed.* Many of these are used without knowledge of their meaning (what is a "rift," for instance?), and incompatible metaphors are frequently mixed, a sure sign that the writer is not interested in what he is saying. Some metaphors now current have been twisted out of their original meaning without those who use them even being aware of the fact. For example, *toe the line* is sometimes written *tow the line*. Another example is *the hammer and the anvil*, now always used with the implication that the anvil gets the worst of it. In real life it is always the anvil that breaks the hammer, never the other way about: a writer who stopped to think what he was saying would be aware of this, and would avoid perverting the original phrase.

OPERATORS OF VERBAL FALSE LIMBS. These save the trouble of picking out appropriate verbs and nouns, and at the same time pad each sentence with extra syllables which give it an appearance of symmetry. Characteristic phrases are *render inoperative, militate against, make contact with, be subjected to, give rise to, give grounds for, have the effect of, play a leading part (role) in, make itself felt, take effect, exhibit a tendency to, serve the purpose of,* etc., etc. The keynote is the elimination of simple verbs. Instead of being a single word, such as *break, stop, spoil, mend, kill,* a verb becomes a *phrase,* made up of a noun or adjective tacked on to some general-purposes verb such as *prove, serve, form, play, render.* In addition, the passive voice is wherever possible used in preference to the active, and noun constructions are used instead of gerunds (*by examination of* instead of *by examining*). The range of verbs is further cut down by means of the *-ize* and *de-* formations, and the banal statements are given an appearance of profundity by means of the *not un-* formation. Simple conjunctions and prepositions are replaced by such phrases as *with respect to, having regard to, the fact that, by dint of, in view of, in the interests of, on the hypothesis that;* and the ends of sentences are saved from anticlimax by such resounding commonplaces as *greatly to be desired, cannot be left out of account, a development to be expected in the near future, deserving of serious consideration, brought to a satisfactory conclusion,* and so on and so forth.

PRETENTIOUS DICTION. Words like *phenomenon, element, individual* (as noun), *objective, categorical, effective, virtual, basic, primary, promote, constitute, exhibit, exploit, utilize, eliminate, liquidate* are used to dress up simple statement and give an air of scientific impartiality to biased judgments. Adjectives like *epoch-making, epic, historic, unforgettable, triumphant, age-old, inevitable, inexorable, veritable,* are used to dignify the sordid processes of international politics, while writing that aims at glorifying war usually takes on an archaic color, its characteristic words being: *realm, throne, chariot, mailed fist, trident, sword, shield, buckler, banner, jackboot, clarion.* Foreign words and expressions such as *cul de sac, ancien régime, deus ex machina, mutatis mutandis, status quo, gleichschaltung, weltanschauung,* are used to give an air of culture and elegance. Except for the useful abbreviations *i.e., e.g.,* and *etc.,* there is no real need for any of the hundreds of foreign phrases now current in English. Bad writers, and especially scientific, political and sociological writers, are nearly always haunted by the notion that Latin or Greek words are grander than Saxon ones, and unnecessary words like *expedite, ameliorate, predict, extraneous, deracinated, clandestine, subaqueous* and hundreds of others constantly gain ground from their Anglo-Saxon opposite numbers.[1] The jargon peculiar to Marxist writing (*hyena, hangman, cannibal, petty bourgeois, these gentry, lacquey, flunkey, mad dog, White Guard,* etc.) consists largely of words and phrases translated from Russian, German or French; but the normal way of coining a new word is to use a Latin or Greek root with the appropriate affix and, where necessary, the *-ize* formation. It is often easier to make up words of this kind (*deregionalize, impermissible, extramarital, nonfragmentary* and so forth) than to think up the English words that will cover one's meaning. The result, in general, is an increase in slovenliness and vagueness.

---

1. An interesting illustration of this is the way in which the English flower names which were in use till very recently are being ousted by Greek ones, *snapdragon* becoming *antirrhinum, forget-me-not* becoming *myosotis, etc.* It is hard to see any practical reason for this change of fashion: it is probably due to an instinctive turning-away from the more homely word and a vague feeling that the Greek word is scientific.

MEANINGLESS WORDS. In certain kinds of writing, particularly in art criticism and literary criticism, it is normal to come across long passages which are almost completely lacking in meaning.[2] Words like *romantic, plastic, values, human, dead, sentimental, natural, vitality,* as used in art criticism, are strictly meaningless, in the sense that they not only do not point to any discoverable object, but are hardly ever expected to do so by the reader. When one critic writes, "The outstanding feature of Mr. X's work is its living quality," while another writes, "The immediately striking thing about Mr. X's work is its peculiar deadness," the reader accepts this as a simple difference of opinion. If words like *black* and *white* were involved, instead of the jargon words *dead* and *living,* he would see at once that language was being used in an improper way. Many political words are similarly abused. The word *Fascism* has now no meaning except in so far as it signifies "something not desirable." The words *democracy, socialism, freedom, patriotic, realistic, justice,* have each of them several different meanings which cannot be reconciled with one another. In the case of a word like *democracy,* not only is there no agreed definition, but the attempt to make one is resisted from all sides. It is almost universally felt that when we call a country democratic we are praising it: consequently the defenders of every kind of régime claim that it is a democracy, and fear that they might have to stop using the word if it were tied down to any one meaning. Words of this kind are often

---

2. Example: "Comfort's catholicity of perception and image, strangely Whitmanesque in range, almost the exact opposite in aesthetic compulsion, continues to evoke that trembling atmospheric accumulative hinting at a cruel, an inexorably serene timelessness . . . Wrey Gardiner scores by aiming at simple bull's-eyes with precision. Only they are not so simple, and through this contented sadness runs more than the surface bitter-sweet of resignation" (*Poetry Quarterly*).

used in a consciously dishonest way. That is, the person who uses them has his own private definition, but allows his hearer to think he means something quite different. Statements like *Marshal Pétain was a true patriot, The Soviet Press is the freest in the world, The Catholic Church is opposed to persecution*, are almost always made with intent to deceive. Other words used in variable meanings, in most cases more or less dishonestly, are: *class, totalitarian, science, progressive, reactionary, bourgeois, equality*.

Now that I have made this catalogue of swindles and perversions, let me give another example of the kind of writing that they lead to. This time it must of its nature be an imaginary one. I am going to translate a passage of good English into modern English of the worst sort. Here is a well-known verse from *Ecclesiastes*:

I returned and saw under the sun, that the race is not to the swift, nor the battle to the strong, neither yet bread to the wise, nor yet riches to men of understanding, nor yet favour to men of skill; but time and chance happeneth to them all.

Here it is in modern English:

Objective consideration of contemporary phenomena compels the conclusion that success or failure in competitive activities exhibits no tendency to be commensurate with innate capacity, but that a considerable element of the unpredictable must invariably be taken into account.

This is a parody, but not a very gross one. Exhibit (3), above, for instance, contains several patches of the same kind of English.

It will be seen that I have not made a full translation. The beginning and ending of the sentence follow the original meaning fairly closely, but in the middle the concrete illustrations—race, battle, bread—dissolve into the vague phrase "success or failure in competitive activities." This had to be so, because no modern writer of the kind I am discussing—no one capable of using phrases like "objective consideration of contemporary phenomena"—would ever tabulate his thoughts in that precise and detailed way. The whole tendency of modern prose is away from concreteness. Now analyse these two sentences a little more closely. The first contains forty-nine words but only sixty syllables, and all its words are those of everyday life. The second contains thirty-eight words of ninety syllables: eighteen of its words are from Latin roots, and one from Greek. The first sentence contains six vivid images, and only one phrase ("time and chance") that could be called vague. The second contains not a single fresh, arresting phrase, and in spite of its ninety syllables it gives only a shortened version of the meaning contained in the first. Yet without a doubt it is the second kind of sentence that is gaining ground in modern English. I do not want to exaggerate. This kind of writing is not yet universal, and outcrops of simplicity will occur here and there in the worst-written page. Still, if you or I were told to write a few lines on the uncertainty of human fortunes, we should probably come much nearer to my imaginary sentence than to the one from *Ecclesiastes*.

As I have tried to show, modern writing at its worst does not consist in picking out words for the sake of their meaning and inventing images in order to make the meaning clearer. It consists in gumming together long strips of words which have already been set in order by someone else, and making the results presentable by sheer humbug. The attraction of this way of writing is that it is easy. It is easier—even quicker, once you have the habit—to say *In my opinion it is not an unjustifiable assumption that* than to say *I think*. If you use ready-made phrases, you not only don't have to hunt about for words; you also don't have to bother with the rhythms of your sentences, since these phrases are generally so arranged as to be more or less euphonious. When you are composing in a hurry—when you are dictating to a stenographer, for instance, or making a public speech—it is natural to fall into a pretentious, Latinized style. Tags like *a consideration which we should do well to bear in mind* or *a conclusion to which all of us would readily assent* will save many a sentence from coming down with a bump. By using stale metaphors, similes and idioms, you save much mental effort, at the cost of leaving your meaning vague, not only for your reader but for yourself. This is the significance of mixed metaphors. The sole aim of a metaphor is to call up a visual image. When these images clash—as in *The Fascist octopus has sung its swan song, the jackboot is thrown into the melting pot*—it can be taken as certain that the writer is not seeing a mental image of the objects he is naming; in other words he is not really thinking. Look again at the examples I gave at the beginning of this essay. Professor Laski (1) uses five negatives in fifty-three words. One of these is superfluous, making nonsense of the whole passage, and in addition there is the slip *alien* for akin, making further nonsense, and several avoidable pieces of clumsiness which increase the general vagueness. Professor Hogben (2) plays ducks and drakes with a battery which is able to write prescriptions, and, while disapproving of the everyday phrase *put up with*, is unwilling to look *egregious* up in the dictionary and see what it means; (3), if one takes an uncharitable attitude towards it, is simply meaningless: probably one could work out its intended meaning by reading the whole of the article in which it occurs. In (4), the writer knows more or less what he wants to say, but an accumulation of stale phrases chokes him like tea leaves blocking a sink. In (5), words and meaning have almost parted company. People who write in this manner usually have a general emotional meaning—they dislike one thing and want to express solidarity with another—but they are not interested in the detail of what they are saying. A scrupulous writer, in every sentence that he writes, will ask himself at least four questions, thus: What am I trying to say? What words will express it? What image or idiom will make it clearer? Is this image fresh enough to have an effect? And he will probably ask himself two more: Could I put it more shortly? Have I said anything that is avoidably ugly? But you are not obliged to go to all this trouble. You can shirk it by simply throwing your mind open and letting the ready-made phrases come crowding in. They will construct your sentences for you—even think your thoughts for you, to a certain extent—and at need they will perform the important service of partially concealing your meaning even from yourself. It is at this point that the special connection between politics and the debasement of language becomes clear.

In our time it is broadly true that political writing is bad writing. Where it is not true, it will generally be found that the writer is some kind of rebel, expressing his private opinions and not a "party line." Orthodoxy, of whatever color, seems to demand a lifeless, imitative style. The political dialects to be found in pamphlets, leading articles, manifestos, White Papers and the speeches of under-secretaries do, of course, vary from party to party, but they are all alike in that one almost never finds in them a fresh, vivid, home-made turn of speech. When one watches some tired hack on the platform mechanically repeating the familiar phrases—*bestial atrocities, iron heel, bloodstained tyranny, free peoples of the world, stand shoulder to shoulder*—one often has a curious feeling that one is not watching a live human being but some kind of dummy: a feeling which suddenly becomes stronger at moments when the light catches the speaker's spectacles and turns them into blank discs which seem to have no eyes behind them. And this is not altogether fanciful. A speaker who uses that kind of phraseology has gone some distance towards turning himself into a machine. The appropriate noises are coming out of his larynx, but his brain is not involved as it would be if he were choosing his words for himself. If the speech he is making is one that he is accustomed to make over and over again, he may be almost unconscious of what he is saying, as one is when one utters the responses in church. And this reduced state of consciousness, if not indispensable, is at any rate favorable to political conformity.

In our time, political speech and writing are largely the defence of the indefensible. Things like the continuance of British rule in India, the Russian purges and deportations, the dropping of the atom bombs on Japan, can indeed be defended, but only by arguments which are too brutal for most people to face, and which do not square with the professed aims of political parties. Thus political language has to consist largely of euphemism, question-begging and sheer cloudy vagueness. Defenceless villages are bombarded from the air, the inhabitants driven out into the countryside, the cattle machine-gunned, the huts set on fire with incendiary bullets: this is called *pacification*. Millions of peasants are robbed of their farms and sent trudging along the roads with no more than they can carry: this is called *transfer of population* or *rectification of frontiers*. People are imprisoned for years without trial, or shot in the back of the neck or sent to die of scurvy in Arctic lumber camps: this is called *elimination of unreliable elements.* Such phraseology is needed if one wants to name things without calling up mental pictures of them. Consider for instance some comfortable English professor defending Russian Totalitarianism. He cannot say outright, "I believe in killing off your opponents when you can get good results by doing so." Probably, therefore, he will say something like this:

> While freely conceding that the Soviet régime exhibits certain features which the humanitarian may be inclined to deplore, we must, I think, agree that a certain curtailment of the right to political opposition is an unavoidable concomitant of transitional periods, and that the rigors which the Russian people have been called upon to undergo have been amply justified in the sphere of concrete achievement.

The inflated style is itself a kind of euphemism. A mass of Latin words falls upon the facts like soft snow, blurring the outlines and covering up all the details. The great enemy of clear language is insincerity. When there is a gap between one's real and one's declared aims, one turns as it were instinctively to long words and exhausted idioms, like a cuttlefish squirting out ink. In our age there is no such thing as "keeping out of politics." All issues are political issues, and politics itself is a mass of lies, evasions, folly, hatred and schizophrenia. When the general atmosphere is bad, language must suffer. I should expect to find—this is a guess which I have not sufficient knowledge to verify—that the German, Russian and Italian languages have all deteriorated in the last ten or fifteen years, as a result of dictatorship.

But if thought corrupts language, language can also corrupt thought. A bad usage can spread by tradition and imitation, even among people who should and do know better. The debased language that I have been discussing is in some ways very convenient. Phrases like *a not unjustifiable assumption, leaves much to be desired, would serve no good purpose, a consideration which we should do well to bear in mind,* are a continuous temptation, a packet of aspirins always at one's elbow. Look back through this essay, and for certain you will find that I have again and again committed the very faults I am protesting against. By this morning's post I have received a pamphlet dealing with conditions in Germany. The author tells me that he "felt impelled" to write it. I open it at random, and here is almost the first sentence that I see: "[The Allies] have an opportunity not only of achieving a radical transformation of Germany's social and political structure in such a way as to avoid a nationalistic reaction in Germany itself, but at the same time of laying the foundations of a co-operative and unified Europe." You see, he "feels impelled" to write—feels, presumably, that he has something new to say—and yet his words, like cavalry horses answering the bugle, group themselves automatically into the familiar dreary pattern. This invasion of one's mind by ready-made phrases (*lay the foundations, achieve a radical transformation*) can only be prevented if one is constantly on guard against them, and every such phrase anaesthetizes a portion of one's brain.

I said earlier that the decadence of our language is probably curable. Those who deny this would argue, if they produced an argument at all, that language merely reflects existing social conditions, and that we cannot influence its development by any direct tinkering with words and constructions. So far as the general tone or spirit of a language goes, this may be true, but it is not true in detail. Silly words and expressions have often disappeared, not through any evolutionary process but owing to the conscious action of a minority. Two recent examples were *explore every avenue* and *leave no stone unturned*, which were killed by the jeers of a few journalists. There is a long list of flyblown metaphors which could similarly be got rid of if enough people would interest themselves in the job; and it should also be possible to laugh the *not un-* formation out of existence,[3] to reduce the amount of Latin and Greek in the average sentence, to drive out foreign phrases and strayed scientific words, and, in general, to make pretentiousness unfashionable. But all these are minor points. The defence of the English language implies more than this, and perhaps it is best to start by saying what it does *not* imply.

To begin with it has nothing to do with archaism, with the salvaging of obsolete words and turns of speech, or with the setting up of a "standard English" which must never be departed from. On the contrary, it is especially concerned with the scrapping of every word or idiom which has outworn its usefulness. It has nothing to do with correct grammar and syntax, which are of no importance so long as one makes one's meaning clear, or with the avoidance of Americanisms, or with having what is called a "good prose style." On the other hand it is not concerned with fake simplicity and the attempt to make written English colloquial. Nor does it even imply in every case preferring the Saxon word to the Latin one, though it does imply using the fewest and shortest words that will cover one's meaning. What is above all needed is to let the meaning

---

3. One can cure oneself of the *not un-* formation by memorizing this sentence: *A not unblack dog was chasing a not unsmall rabbit across a not ungreen field.*

choose the word, and not the other way about. In prose, the worst thing one can do with words is to surrender to them. When you think of a concrete object, you think wordlessly, and then, if you want to describe the thing you have been visualizing you probably hunt about till you find the exact words that seem to fit it. When you think of something abstract you are more inclined to use words from the start, and unless you make a conscious effort to prevent it, the existing dialect will come rushing in and do the job for you, at the expense of blurring or even changing your meaning. Probably it is better to put off using words as long as possible and get one's meaning as clear as one can through pictures or sensations. Afterwards one can choose—not simply *accept*—the phrases that will best cover the meaning, and then switch round and decide what impression one's words are likely to make on another person. This last effort of the mind cuts out all stale or mixed images, all prefabricated phrases, needless repetitions, and humbug and vagueness generally. But one can often be in doubt about the effect of a word or a phrase, and one needs rules that one can rely on when instinct fails. I think the following rules will cover most cases:

1. Never use a metaphor, simile or other figure of speech which you are used to seeing in print.
2. Never use a long word where a short one will do.
3. If it is possible to cut a word out, always cut it out.
4. Never use the passive where you can use the active.
5. Never use a foreign phrase, a scientific word or a jargon word if you can think of an everyday English equivalent.
6. Break any of these rules sooner than say anything outright barbarous.

These rules sound elementary, and so they are, but they demand a deep change in attitude in anyone who has grown used to writing in the style now fashionable. One could keep all of them and still write bad English, but one could not write the kind of stuff that I quoted in those five specimens at the beginning of this article.

I have not here been considering the literary use of language, but merely language as an instrument for expressing and not for concealing or preventing thought. Stuart Chase and others have come near to claming that all abstract words are meaningless, and have used this as a pretext for advocating a kind of political quietism. Since you don't know what Fascism is, how can you struggle against Fascism? One need not swallow such absurdities as this, but one ought to recognize that the present political chaos is connected with the decay of language, and that one can probably bring about some improvement by starting at the verbal end. If you simplify your English, you are freed from the worst follies of orthodoxy. You cannot speak any of the necessary dialects, and when you make a stupid remark its stupidity will be obvious, even to yourself. Political language—and with variations this is true of all political parties, from Conservatives to Anarchists—is designed to make lies sound truthful and murder respectable, and to give an appearance of solidity to pure wind. One cannot change this all in a moment, but one can at least change one's own habits, and from time to time one can even, if one jeers loudly enough, send some worn-out and useless phrase—some *jackboot, Achilles' heel, hotbed, melting pot, acid test, veritable inferno* or other lump of verbal refuse—into the dustbin where it belongs.

—1946

NOTES

FOLLIES OF ORTHODOXY

1. Laurence Brander, *George Orwell* (London: Longman's, Green and Co., 1956), 27.

2. Ibid., 35.

3. George Orwell, "Politics and the English Language," in Orwell, *A Collection of Essays* (New York: Harcourt, 1970), 157.

4. Brander, *Orwell*, 199.

5. Ibid., 198.

6. Ibid., 190.

7. Ibid.

8. Edward Bernays, *Propaganda* (New York: H. Liveright, 1928), 71.

9. Al Gore, *The Assault on Reason* (New York: Penguin Press, 2007), 94.

10. Ibid., 94–95.

11. Liang Congjie, *The Great Thoughts of China* (New York: Wiley, 1996), 221.

12. Mao Zedong, "On Coalition Government," from *Selected Works*, vol. 3 (Beijing, China: 1966), 316–317.

13. Robert J. Lifton, *Thought Reform and the Psychology of Totalism* (New York: W. W. Norton and Co., 1963), 390.

14. Ibid., 391.

15. Orville Schell, *The China Reader: The Reform Years* (New York: Vintage, New York, 1999), 265.

16. Ibid., 266.

17. Ibid.
18. Lifton, *Thought Reform*, 397.
19. Gore, *Assault on Reason*, 252.

WORDS IN A TIME OF WAR

1. Orwell, George, "The Prevention of Literature" (1946), *The Orwell Reader: Fiction, Essays and Reportage* (New York: Harcourt, 1956), 371.

WHAT ORWELL DIDN'T KNOW ABOUT
THE BRAIN, THE MIND, AND LANGUAGE

1. See George Lakoff, Marc Ettlinger, and Sam Ferguson, "Bush Is Not Incompetent," June 25, 2006, at http://www.rockridgeinstitute.org/research/lakoff/incompetent, and George Lakoff and John Halpin, "Framing Katrina," October 20, 2005 (reprinted from *The American Prospect Online*), at http://www.rockridgeinstitute.org/research/lakoff/framingkatrina.

THE NEW FRONTIER

1. James Moore and Wayne Slater, *Bush's Brain: How Karl Rove Made George W. Bush Presidential* (Hoboken, NJ: John Wiley and Sons, 2003); and James Moore and Wayne Slater, *The Architect: Karl Rove and the Master Plan for Absolute Power* (New York: Random House, 2006).
2. Tom Pyszczynski, Sheldon Solomon, and Jeff Greenberg, *In the Wake of 9/11: The Psychology of Terror* (Washington, DC: American Psychological Association, 2003).
3. Drew Westen, *The Political Brain: The Role of Emotion in Deciding the Fate of the Nation* (New York: PublicAffairs, 2007).
4. See http://livingroomcandidate.movingimage.us/election/index.php?nav_action=election&nav_subaction=overview&campaign_id=173.
5. Westen, *The Political Brain*.

BLACK AND WHITE, OR GRAY

1. Jarosław Kaczyński, speech at Law and Justice Congress, June 4, 2006.

2. Jarosław and Lech Kaczyński had been active in the opposition since the 1970s and played a major role in the roundtable negotiations of 1989 and the subsequent political transformation.

3. Having learned of his victory, he stood at attention in front of his brother and said: "Mister Chairman, I report mission completed." The event was televised live.

4. "We are the moral revolution," Law and Justice electoral slogan, 2005.

5. *Głos Wybrzeża*, June 18, 2003.

6. Interview with RMF FM radio, March 2005.

7. Ibid., September 22, 2005.

8. I was among those journalists who refused to submit a lustration statement. The lustration law was eventually thrown out by the constitutional court.

9. Interview for *Gazeta Polska*, March 29, 2006.

10. Speech in Parliament, February 17, 2006.

11. Speech at Law and Justice Congress, June 4, 2006.

12. *Gazeta Wyborcza*, May 13, 2006.

13. Interview on Polish radio, Channel 1, May 15, 2007.

14. Interview on fundamentalist Catholic broadcaster radio Marya, March 16, 2006.

15. Interview for the Polish edition of *Newsweek*, March 26, 2006.

16. Interview for *Polityka* weekly, March 25, 2006.

17. In its heyday, PZPR had 3 million members, in a nation of 36 million.

18. His principled stance is not shared by the League of Polish Families. The All-Polish Youth, its youth movement until it was disowned in 2006, is composed mainly of skinheads, and the League overtly considers itself the successor of the prewar, anti-Semitic, and fascistic National Democratic Party.

19. This topic, though of paramount importance, cannot be discussed in the framework of this brief essay.

20. *Gazeta Wyborcza,* September 6, 2006. These quotes are characteristic of the Kaczyński brothers' utter disregard for the courts—again, another topic that cannot be discussed here for lack of space.

21. It eventually transpired that Tusk's grandfather, a Polish political prisoner in a Nazi camp, had indeed volunteered for the Wehrmacht, in order to desert to the Allies, as he did one month after having been incorporated into the German army.

22. TVN "Co z ta Polską" program, November 17, 2005.

23. Speech in Gdańsk, October 1, 2006.

24. His deputy minister of justice, Andrzej Kryże, had as a judge sentenced oppositionists in the 1970s and 1980s. On the other hand, Józef Medyk, a judge who had ruled that participants in a strike against martial law were innocent, was recently removed from his position as head of the Electoral Commission for Warsaw, after having made a ruling in a local elections case that countered the government's wishes.

25. *Gazeta Wyborcza,* February 5, 2006.

26. Speech in Parliament, June 19, 2006.

AFTER THE FALWELLIANS

1. George Orwell, "Politics and the English Language," in Orwell, *A Collection of Essays* (New York: Harcourt, 1970).

2. These days, theologically conservative and orthodox Protestants are all called, and most call themselves, "evangelicals." This includes independent Baptists such as Falwell's church people, who, until the late 1990s were called, and called themselves, fundamentalists, and pentecostal and charismatic Christians. In this essay, I use the term "fundamentalist" to refer to evangelicals formerly known as fundamentalists and to evangelicals who are socially as well as theologically conservative and actively identify with and participate in religious right politics.

3. See http://www.thomasnelson.com/Consumer/product_detail.asp?sku=0718003586 and click on "View Sample Video."

4. Geoffrey Nunberg, *Talking Right* (New York: PublicAffairs, 2006), 3, 4–5.

5. See Susan Harding, *The Book of Jerry Falwell* (Princeton: Princeton University Press, 2000), *passim*.

6. Ron Suskind, "Without a Doubt," *New York Times Magazine*, October 17, 2004.

7. Richard John Neuhaus, *The Naked Public Square* (Grand Rapids, MI: Eerdmans, 1984).

8. The dynamics described here have, of course, happened before in American history, most recently and across much the same subcultural and political divide, in the 1940s and 1950s, when social moderates mobilized and emerged out of the fundamentalist fold, calling themselves "evangelicals" to distinguish themselves from their right-wing brethren.

9. Frances FitzGerald, "The Evangelical Surprise," *New York Review of Books*, April 26, 2007.

10. See http://www.creationcare.org/respoes/faq.php.

11. See http://environment.harvard.edu/religion/religion/christianity/projects/evangelical_envt.html.

12. See http://whatwouldjesusdrive.org/intro.php.

13. The phrase "What Would Jesus Do?" was coined by Charles Sheldon, an early twentieth-century Congregational social gospel and prohibitionist preacher in his best-selling book, *In His Steps* (cited by Richard Wightman Fox, *Jesus in America* [San Francisco: HarperSanFrancisco, 2004], 278–282).

14. See http://www.christiansandclimate.org/.

15. For explicit distancing, see http://www.chriiansandclimate.org/faq.

16. Steve Thorngate, "False Stewardship," *Sojourners* (August 2006), 7.

17. Some film review titles: "Al Gore, Preacher Man" *(Christianity Today);* "Born-Again" *(Guardian);* "Al Gore's Apocalyptic Environmentalism" *(San Francisco Chronicle).*

18. James Morone, *Hellfire Nation* (New Haven: Yale University Press, 2003), 14.

19. Quotes are from the Al Gore documentary *An Inconvenient Truth*, 2006.

20. Sacvan Bercovitch, *The American Jeremiad* (Madison: University of Wisconsin Press, 1978), 23.

21. Stephenie Hendricks, *Divine Destruction* (Hoboken, NJ: Melville House, 2005), 22–23.

22. The film trailer for *An Inconvenient Truth*, by speeding everything up, actually performs the apocalyptic better than the movie, which plays as much to reason, logic, and statistics as to jeremiad rhetoric in making the case for urgency in the face of impending doom.

23. William Connolly, *Why I Am Not a Secularist* (Minneapolis: University of Minnesota Press, 1999).

24. Orwell, "Notes on the Way" (1940), reprinted in *The Collected Essays, Journalism, and Letters of George Orwell*, vol. 2 (New York: Harcourt, Brace and World, 1968).

25. Ibid.

26. This is Orwell's gloss of what Marx said in his *Contribution to the Critique of Hegel's Philosophy of Right:* "Religious suffering is, at one and the same time, the expression of real suffering and a protest against real suffering. Religion is the sigh of the oppressed creature, the heart of a heartless world, and the soul of soulless conditions. It is the opium of the people."

WELCOME TO THE INFOTAINMENT FREAK SHOW

1. Neil Postman, *Amusing Ourselves to Death: Public Discourse in the Age of Show Business* (New York: Penguin, 1985), 98.

NOTES

NEITHER SNOW, NOR RAIN, NOR HEAT, NOR GLOOM OF NIGHT. . .

1. Richard R. John, *Spreading the News: The American Postal System from Franklin to Morse* (Cambridge: Harvard University Press, 1995).

WHAT I DIDN'T KNOW

1. Drew Westen, *The Political Brain: The Role of Emotion in Deciding the Fate of the Nation* (New York: PublicAffairs, 2007).
2. Ibid.

Geoffrey Cowan, a former director of the Voice of America and dean of the USC Annenberg School for Communication, is a university professor at the University of Southern California, where he holds the Annenberg Family Chair in Communication Leadership and teaches courses in media, law, and society, and in public diplomacy. An award-winning, best-selling author, his books include *See No Evil: The Backstage Battle over Sex and Violence on Television* and *The People v. Clarence Darrow: The Bribery Trial of America's Greatest Lawyer*. He lives in Los Angeles, California, with his wife.

Mark Danner has written on foreign policy and political and military conflict for two decades, covering Central America, Haiti, the Balkans, and the Middle East. A former staff writer for the *New Yorker*, he has written for the *New York Review of Books*, the *New York Times*, and many other publications. His most recent books are *Torture and Truth: America, Abu Ghraib and the War on Terror*, and *The Secret Way to War: The Downing Street Memo and the Iraq War's Buried History*. Danner is professor of journalism at the University of California at Berkeley and James Clarke Chace Professor of Politics and Literature at Bard College. He lives in Northern California and New York City.

Farnaz Fassihi is senior Middle East correspondent for the *Wall Street Journal*, based in Beirut, Lebanon. She started traveling to Iraq in 2002 when Saddam Hussein was still in power and served as the *Journal*'s Baghdad bureau chief from 2003–2006. Prior to that she worked as a roving foreign correspondent for the *Newark Star-Ledger* and as a reporter for the *Providence Journal* in Rhode Island. She is currently working on a book about her time in Iraq.

Frances FitzGerald is the author of several books, including *Fire in the Lake: The Vietnamese and the Americans in Vietnam*, which won a Pulitzer Prize and the National Book Award. She is a frequent contributor to the *New Yorker* and has written for numerous publications, including the *New York Review of Books*, the *New York Times Magazine, Esquire, Architectural Digest, Islands*, and *Rolling Stone*. She lives in Manhattan.

Konstanty Gebert, a former Solidarity activist, is a columnist and international reporter for the Polish newspaper *Gazeta Wyborcza*, and a frequent contributor to international media. The author of eight books, he has served as a visiting professor at a number of American universities. He lives in Warsaw.

Susan Harding is professor of anthropology at the University of California, Santa Cruz. She writes about social movements, language, and cultural politics. Her recent publications include *The Book of Jerry Falwell: Fundamentalist Language and Politics* (2000) and the coedited volume *Histories of the Future* (2005). She lives in Santa Cruz, California.

Martin Kaplan holds the Norman Lear Chair in Entertainment, Media and Society at the USC Annenberg School. A former deputy campaign manager and chief speechwriter for Vice President Walter F. Mondale, Kaplan was also a Disney Studios film executive, screenwriter, and producer. A Harvard summa cum laude in molecular biology, he won a

Marshall Scholarship to study English at Cambridge University before earning a Ph.D. in modern thought and literature from Stanford University. He lives in Los Angeles.

George Lakoff is Goldman Distinguished Professor of Cognitive Science and Linguistics at the University of California, Berkeley, and senior fellow at the Rockridge Institute. He is the author of *Moral Politics, Don't Think of an Elephant!, Whose Freedom?* and *Thinking Points* (with the Rockridge Institute). His next book, *The Political Mind*, will be published by Viking/Penguin in 2008.

Nicholas Lemann is dean of the Columbia University Graduate School of Journalism and a staff writer for the *New Yorker*. His most recent book is *Redemption: The Last Battle of the Civil War*. He lives with his family in New York City.

Michael Massing is a contributing editor of the *Columbia Journalism Review*. A frequent contributor to the *New York Review of Books*, he is the author of *Now They Tell Us: The American Press and Iraq*. He lives in New York City.

Victor Navasky, publisher emeritus of the *Nation*, where he served as editor and then publisher, was formerly an editor at the *New York Times Magazine* and wrote a monthly column about the publishing business (In Cold Print) for the *New York Times Book Review*. He is the author of several nonfiction books, most recently *A Matter of Opinion*, winner of the 2005 George Polk Book Award. Navasky is director of the George Delacorte Center for Magazine Journalism at Columbia University, where he is chairman of the *Columbia Journalism Review*. He lives in New York City with his wife.

Aryeh Neier has been the president of the Open Society Institute since 1993. Previously, he was executive director of Human Rights Watch and, before that, of the American Civil Liberties Union. The author of six books, he lives in Manhattan.

Alice O'Connor is an associate professor of history at the University of California, Santa Barbara. She is the author of *Poverty Knowledge: Social Science, Social Policy, and the Poor in Twentieth-Century U.S. History* (2001) and *Social Science for What? Philanthropy and the Social Question in a World Turned Rightside Up* (2007), among other publications. Before joining the UCSB faculty, she was a program officer at the Ford Foundation and the Social Science Research Council. She lives in Santa Barbara, California.

Francine Prose is the author of eleven novels, including *Blue Angel*, which was nominated for a 2000 National Book Award. Her most recent book is *Reading Like a Writer*. Her stories, reviews, and essays have appeared in the *Atlantic Monthly*, *Harper's*, *Best American Short Stories*, the *New Yorker*, the *New York Times*, and numerous other publications. A 1999 Director's Fellow of the New York Public Library's Center for Scholars and Writers, she is a contributing editor of *Harper's Magazine* and *Bomb* magazine and writes regularly on art for the *Wall Street Journal*. Her novel, *A Changed Man,* was the first winner of the Dayton Literary Peace Prize. The winner of a Guggenheim Fellowship, a Fulbright fellowship, two NEA grants, and a PEN translation prize, she is currently president of PEN American Center, and teaches at Bard College.

David Rieff is a contributing writer to the *New York Times Magazine*. He is the author of eight books, including *A Bed for the Night: Humanitarianism in Crisis*, *At the Point of a Gun: Democratic Dreams and Armed Inter-*

vention and, most recently, *Swimming in a Sea of Death: A Son's Memoir.* He lives in New York.

Orville Schell, author of more than a dozen books, has written for many journals and magazines, including *Wired,* the *New York Review of Books,* the *New Yorker, Harper's,* the *New York Times,* the *Atlantic,* and *Newsweek.* Formerly the dean of the Graduate School of Journalism at the University of California at Berkeley, he is currently the Arthur Ross Director of the Asia Society's Center on U.S.-China relations. He divides his time between Manhattan and Berkeley, California.

George Soros is chairman of Soros Fund Management LLC, and founder of the Open Society Institute. Born in Budapest in 1930, he survived the Nazi occupation and fled Communist Hungary in 1947 for England, where he graduated from the London School of Economics. Soros has established a network of philanthropic organizations that are active in more than fifty countries. Soros is the author of nine books, including, most recently, *The Age of Fallibility.* His articles and essays on politics, society, and economics regularly appear in major newspapers and magazines around the world. He lives in New York.

András Szántó is a writer, researcher, and consultant to cultural and philanthropic organizations. He is coauthor and editor of four books and has written for the *New York Times,* the *Boston Globe,* the *Los Angeles Times,* and the *American Prospect,* among other publications. He is a senior lecturer at the Sotheby's Institute of Art in New York and director of the NEA Arts Journalism Institute at Columbia University. Born in Budapest, he lives in Brooklyn with his wife and son.

Drew Westen, a clinical, personality, and political psychologist, is a professor in the Departments of Psychology and Psychiatry at Emory

University. Founder of Westen Strategies, a political and corporate consulting firm, he advises Democratic leaders and candidates. The author of *The Political Brain: The Role of Emotion in Deciding the Fate of the Nation*, he lives in Atlanta, Georgia.

Patricia Williams is the John Dohr Professor of Law at Columbia University. She writes the column Diary of a Mad Law Professor for the *Nation*. She lives in New York.

This anthology is a companion to "There You Go Again: Orwell Comes to America," a conference at the New York Public Library on November 7, 2007. Both this book and the conference have received support from the Open Society Institute. More information on the Orwell project can be found at www.thereyougoagain.org.

The Open Society Institute works to build vibrant and tolerant democracies whose governments are accountable to their citizens. To achieve its mission, OSI seeks to shape public policies that assure greater fairness in political, legal, and economic systems and safeguard fundamental rights. On a local level, OSI implements a range of initiatives to advance justice, education, public health, and independent media. At the same time, OSI builds alliances across borders and continents on issues such as corruption and freedom of information. OSI places a high priority on protecting and improving the lives of marginalized people and communities.

PublicAffairs is a publishing house founded in 1997. It is a tribute to the standards, values, and flair of three persons who have served as mentors to countless reporters, writers, editors, and book people of all kinds, including me.

I.F. Stone, proprietor of *I. F. Stone's Weekly*, combined a commitment to the First Amendment with entrepreneurial zeal and reporting skill and became one of the great independent journalists in American history. At the age of eighty, Izzy published *The Trial of Socrates*, which was a national bestseller. He wrote the book after he taught himself ancient Greek.

Benjamin C. Bradlee was for nearly thirty years the charismatic editorial leader of *The Washington Post*. It was Ben who gave the *Post* the range and courage to pursue such historic issues as Watergate. He supported his reporters with a tenacity that made them fearless and it is no accident that so many became authors of influential, best-selling books.

Robert L. Bernstein, the chief executive of Random House for more than a quarter century, guided one of the nation's premier publishing houses. Bob was personally responsible for many books of political dissent and argument that challenged tyranny around the globe. He is also the founder and longtime chair of Human Rights Watch, one of the most respected human rights organizations in the world.

• • •

For fifty years, the banner of Public Affairs Press was carried by its owner Morris B. Schnapper, who published Gandhi, Nasser, Toynbee, Truman, and about 1,500 other authors. In 1983, Schnapper was described by *The Washington Post* as "a redoubtable gadfly." His legacy will endure in the books to come.

Peter Osnos, *Founder and Editor-at-Large*